HOW TO ANALYZE PEOPLE WITH DARK PSYCHOLOGY

A Way to Enter into The Existing Invisible Reality Game of The Most Diverse Hidden Attitudes The Individual Possesses, Unnoticed by Some And Dominated by Others, Using Totally Infallible Techniques.

Erick Milton

© Copyright 2021- All rights reserved.

Table of Contents

Introduction

Every person is different in terms of psychology, but all of them have certain elements that are almost identical. No one knows these elements better than a dark person. He knows what pushes us, pulls us, and how to make us feel bad. It's amazing how a specific psychological move can be the most effective way to control a person. In this article, I will try to tell you how to analyze people with dark psychology, how they think, what are their methods, and what moves they use. The information I'm giving you is based on my personal experience.

First of all, it's important to know that dark personality are interested in the positive results of their actions and they don't care about the feelings of the people around them. That's why a person who uses such tactics in his life needs a lot of self-control and ignoring. This is the first step to analyzing people with dark psychology. When you begin to understand the methods and moves of a person, then you know what to expect from him.

Everyone has their favorite tactics of controlling persons. Here I am going to talk about those that many dark personalities use.

The following techniques are used by dark personalities:

1. They try to make you an accomplice in their dirty deeds.

Never accept this, you should never stoop to such low levels. If you do, then you will become their slave. A good way to do this is to pretend that you are on their side and they need to trust you. Then when they least expect it, turn against them and fight for what is right.

2.   To show the other side of a person.

This is one of the most effective techniques of dark personalities it makes us doubt our inner judge that people seem good or bad from the beginning. This helps them gain our trust more easily.

3.   To complement in a non-interested manner.

This is the most effective method of conquering people, they need to see that you have a lot of problems and you are looking for help in every person you can find. The main thing here is to convince the other person that you are helpless and he is your only hope, then he will think, "Why so much effort if he will come to me willingly?" and will be on your side.

4.   To ignore and show that you are better than others.

Another similar method to make people stand at attention. When you want to be an important person, don't talk to everyone, they will look at you as if you were some kind of a celebrity and they might be afraid to talk to you. This works perfectly for those who love such things. The best way to use this tactic is when the other person wants something from you, especially when he wants your help or trust.

5.   They show their dark side, pretending to be a good person.

This is a very effective move that many dark personalities use, they try to hide their bad deeds and pretend to be a good person until they get what they want. When you see how they act in different situations, you will notice that something is not right with them. This will give you an advantage in information gathering and later when you are analyzing them.

For example, a dark-personality person doesn't mind if he breaks a girl's heart. He can be glad that he coped with his business. After all, it's not his fault if she chose to trust him and like him at all. The main thing is that everything went out the way it was supposed to go.

And after breaking her heart, he can do any amount of nice things for her until she forgets about him. Once they get back together, he won't be afraid to break her heart again.

The main goal of dark psychology is to achieve your goal and have no regrets about anything. There are no emotions here. You're a puppet in this game, but that's the way you like it. The only thing you should be afraid of is being sad when the time comes for you to break someone's heart and stand on their side and appreciate the beauty of this situation. That's enough self-analysis for today.

CHAPTER 1:

Short History of Dark Manipulation

There are many things in the world that people can try to use for their ends, but few are as versatile and increasingly popular as dark manipulation. The concept of dark manipulation is easy to understand, and the effects it can have on a person's mind are also relatively straightforward, but one should never underestimate how far a sinister individual might go to achieve their goals. As long as there have been humans, there has been dark manipulation. In the past, it was not considered a particularly special power or skill, more of a tool of the trade for anyone who wanted to get ahead.

For example, a politician might use it to persuade voters to vote for them, while an investor might use it to bend a businessman's will so that he would sign an unfair contract or donate money to the politician's campaign. In such examples, the dark manipulator is using his power to gain a personal advantage, whether that's a higher position in society or just financial and social security for themselves. This sort of dark manipulation has always been present in human society and is really not much different from how people use the same powers today, but some have begun to use their powers for more ambitious purposes.

Some use their powers of persuasion to gain power for themselves and to bend the world into the shape they want it to be, while others use their powers to do good for others. In any case, those who use their power wisely can often achieve great things and help change society for the better. This is by no means an exhaustive history of dark manipulation, but simply a brief overview of some important events in its history. This overview focuses on the history of dark manipulation and its uses, rather than any individual wielders of dark power as much of that information is not available. The early years The first evidence that suggests that people were using their talents for purposes other than self-advancement comes from a time so long ago that no one can accurately put a date on it, but archeologists have found traces of an ancient civilization in southern North America where there was a clear division between the haves and the have-nots.

Centuries before even the Aztecs or Mayans were a threat to the region, this civilization was already showing signs of its eventual decline and slow extinction. Few records survive from this time and it is not clear exactly what role dark manipulation would have played in its collapse, but it is clear that there was widespread use of dark powers in both their society and military. It is thought that the head of this society ruled through fear and maintained order through brutal displays of power, but as no communication has been found from this pre-Aztec society, it will probably never be known for certain if that was true.

In ancient Japan, the use of dark manipulation among the samurai was widespread and well-known. It was not seen as shameful to use one's talents in this way among any social class or any situation. The morality of using one's talents in such a way was not questioned at all, something that seems strange to people living in the modern world. This attitude towards dark manipulation persisted even after the fall of the samurai and into the twentieth century when it was finally outlawed. For centuries people used their talents for everything from personal gain to military conquest and social engineering. For many people, dark manipulation was simply a way of life.

The Modern Era: The Age of Enlightenment

This attitude came to change in the nineteenth century, during the Age of Enlightenment. During this time, scientific thinking was often more valued than old religious beliefs, and magic and dark manipulation were frowned upon. In a way, this period represents a sort of moral revolution for many Westerners. Traditional ideas and prejudices were cast off and there was a new emphasis on rationality, science, and progress that led to major cultural changes that persist today. The Industrial Revolution during this time made it harder for people to use magic as a way to gain power, and there was a growing mistrust of its benefits. This era is also notable for major advances in technology and medicine that allowed many more people to live longer, healthier lives. The scientific community's growing skepticism about the usefulness of dark manipulation led them to study it scientifically, with varying degrees of success. Many of the earliest books on applied dark manipulation were written during this time, and the scientific understanding of dark manipulation grew significantly throughout the end of the nineteenth century. As a result, many new technologies were developed that allowed people to perform the same kinds of tasks that they had been using magic for in previous eras.

People using their talents for commercial purposes led to the widespread use of mind control and brainwashing. The brainwashing was not quite as effective, but the results often looked the same. Using such technological advances to replace dark manipulation meant that many people lost their jobs and had to find new ways to make a living, driving down wages for others in the process. The rise of technology and its reliance on electricity led to increased use of power grids in cities. This centralized power led some people to wonder if they could use dark manipulation to shut down or even control entire cities. This power was not completely unprecedented, but it had never been attempted on such a large scale before and many people were afraid to even try. Yet the potential benefits were so great that over time this sort of technology became widespread.

As technology continued to grow, dark manipulation became less common as people used it less and less often. The impression that dark manipulation might be disappearing altogether led the scientific community to further study the field to make sure that no research was lost. The study of dark manipulation continued to advance, and during the early twentieth century, it saw the development of many new theories and technologies. Many people believed that dark manipulation was dying out in favor of more advanced technologies, but this was not true. Rather, dark manipulation had simply become so commonplace that few people even noticed. People had redesigned their cities to incorporate dark manipulation into everything from the street lamps to the traffic signals, making nighttime crime nearly impossible.

CHAPTER 2:

How and When to Use Dark Psychology

Dark psychology is the practice of engaging in activities that are viewed as unethical and immoral to promote or elevate one's self. Practitioners of dark psychology will use things like manipulation, coercion, and intimidation to get the desired result. Unlike other types of psychological practices, this type is almost exclusively used for one's gain and may be involved in criminal activity.

The most common time to utilize dark psychology is when you are trying to manipulate someone into doing something they would not have otherwise done. For example, if you want someone to give you money or something else valuable, then Dark Psychology can be used to coerce them into doing so. Dark psychology is also commonly used by 'bad guys' in movies and literature to coerce the good characters into doing something they otherwise would not have done.

How to Use Dark Psychology

There are many ways to use dark psychology in everyday life. Some ways that people practice this type of psychology include: lying, cheating, bullying, manipulation, stealing, and even killing. You can use Dark Psychology for almost anything you want. The key to using dark psychology effectively is to be smart about it. You have to know when, where, and how to use it. Dark psychology is most effective if used by people who are typically trusting and kind. These types of people will often comply with requests made by someone they know or even like, even if it is not in their best interests or goes against their morals. People who are not trusting, however, will not be so easily manipulated by Dark Psychology.

Dark Psychology can be used in a variety of ways to manipulate someone. One thing you can do is lie to them and tell them that something bad will happen if they do not comply with what you are asking. For example, if you want someone to give you some money, threaten to punch them in the face, or even just tell them that your friend is outside ready to beat them up if they don't give it to you. Another tactic is to tell them you will be upset with them if they do not comply. For example, if you want someone to clean your room for you, just tell them how disappointed you will be if they do not. If the person is the type to be easily influenced and likes pleasing others, then this is a good way to use Dark Psychology.

Dark Psychology can also be used without saying a word. You can simply use your facial expression and body language to show the person you are angry with them or even disappointed in them. This type of psychology works great for people who are not so easily influenced by words alone. You simply have to intimidate the other person into doing what you want. You can look at them with a mean or angry face, just stare at them, or even walk towards them angrily. Most people will be intimidated in these situations and comply with your request.

Another way you can use dark psychology is to threaten someone into doing what you want. If you tell another person that you are going to do bad things to them if they do not comply, then most people will be very scared and likely comply with your request. Threatening another person is a very effective way of getting what you want without having to use words or intimidation. Threatening people is also a common practice in movies and books to show how bad the dark person is.

You can also use Dark Psychology by stealing something from someone. For example, if you want someone to give you a ride somewhere, steal their car keys and then make them drive you there. Or take something of theirs that they want back from you because they will most likely comply with your request to get it back. Stealing is another very common tactic used in movies and books to show how evil the dark person is.

One of the most effective ways to use Dark Psychology is by physically harming someone. This type of psychology works best when used on people who fear physical harm. For example, if you want someone to give you a lot of money, kill their dog or something else that they love and it will make them do what you want. Another way you can use this type of psychology is in self-defense. If you are in danger, you can defend yourself against your attacker by killing the person instead. This will probably satisfy your immediate need for safety and be effective in gaining compliance from your attacker.

Dark Psychology can also be used to try and create an appealing image of yourself. For example, if you want girls to like you, just tell them that you are a very dangerous or evil person who does not care about hurting people. This is another very common tactic used in movies and books to show how bad a character is.

As you can see, there are a lot of ways to utilize Dark Psychology and it can work in almost any situation. The key is to just be smart about using it and not abuse it. Use it on people who deserve it or you could go to jail. You can even get caught by the police if you use Dark Psychology against someone else, or yourself for that matter.

CHAPTER 3:

How to Learn to Read Eyes

The eyes are said to be the windows to our soul and our thoughts. There is so much that you can tell just by looking at a person's eyes and the various movements that they make. The reason why you will be so interested in decoding the meaning is the fact that humans will always hide their emotions depending on the different situations.

To be a stellar analyzer, follow the steps outlined below.

1. **The first thing that you need to establish is your reason for wanting to analyze someone.** Do you want to know whether they are lying to you or trying to validate their authenticity? It doesn't matter if you are dealing with a stranger or not. The rules are the same.

2. **Once you establish your reason, the next step is baselining the eyes.** The baseline process involves establishing how a person's eyes are behaving in a normal and non-threatening situation. Do this by asking casual and neutral topics such as what they think about the weather, what they would like to drink, as well as movie and hobby preferences. The baselining questions should be no-brainers and something that nobody would really lie about. Take note of how the eyes behave as you are having this talk, and you have your baseline.

3. **The next step is looking for any signs of eye deviation from the baseline.** For instance, if you are on a first date, you must keep tabs on the conversations and topics that make the other party's eyes deviate from the baseline.

4. These are potential red-flags, and you may want to dig a little deeper. Psychologists and the FBI use this tactic all the time, and they are able to establish which questions they need to dig deeper on.

In the case you realize any baseline deviations, take note of if it takes the form of:

Eye-blocking

Eye blocking often happens when a person feels threatened, or when they are repulsed by something that they see or hear. Basically, this is an indication of a very uncomfortable situation, mostly due to disbelief or innate disagreement. Some people display eye blocking by rapid blinking while others take to rubbing the eyes using different forms. Learning to read eye-blocking can help you realize when you have repulsed people, enabling you to make it up or change the topic immediately.

Many years ago, I was out on a date with a person that I liked and felt instant chemistry. As we got to know each other, I may have said something demeaning about people who opted to go for a divorce rather than staying and fighting for their marriage. I was trying to come off as a keeper, and I missed his sudden change of demeanor, which involved a lot of eye rubbing. Turns out, he had married young and had already been divorced once. Needless to say, we never went out on a second date. If I had known what I know now, I would have potentially saved the situation

Squinting

People will often squint their eyes if they do not like you or something that you are saying. This behavior is similar to eye-blocking, and you should address it quickly or clarify whatever it is that you have said before it gets worse.

Eye Positions

Understanding eye positions is immensely important in the analysis process, and it will tell you a lot with minimum effort.

You can analyze these eye movements when doing cross-examinations, interviews, or generally when a person is talking to you. From this analysis, you can tell whether a person is lying to you or not.

Right eye movements are associated with truth while left eye movements are associated with lies/making things up. You must realize that human beings will always have a strong desire to be liked and accepted, and sometimes creating a façade of who they seem like the best option. Regardless of the content through which you are analyzing a person, knowing this technique will help you know who you are dealing with.

When a person is talking about a past event, they often rely on stored memories which they can vividly remember and describe. The memories are said to be on the left side of the brain, and that is why eye movements are to their upper left (Your right if you are directly facing them). However, if a person is just being deceptive and has to come up with a fake story, the eyes will shift to the left. The same case applies to when they are talking about remembered sounds such as conversations they claim to have had in the past.

When a person is having an internal dialogue/debate, they will most likely glance at the lower left. However, remembering a feeling will have them glance on the lower right

Note that movement of the eyes is considered to be one of the most accurate methods of analyzing a person/situation, although it is not fool-proof. You have to pay very close attention to the movements and put them in the context of the discussion to avoid making wrong judgments. In most cases, you have to associate the movement with the exact word or sentence that a person is saying. Consider the following scenario:

A person may be telling the truth about an incident and add bits of lies in between. For example, a statement like "I graduated in business and commerce from Harvard University" may have two parts. It may be true that indeed the person graduated in business and commerce, with the only exception being that they did not attend Harvard. If you are keen enough, you may notice the sudden shift in eye movements which will be red flags. If you are not sure about what you have observed, it is prudent to ask follow-up questions at this point. For example, you can ask the person to tell you all about Harvard and what their experience was in the institution. Such a question requires a lengthy answer, and you will be able to observe eye movements much more accurately at this point.

Sideways Glances

When a person is giving sideways glances, it is often an indication that they are uncertain, and often an indication of nervousness. You may want to ask follow-up questions since this may be a sign of deception. Again, it really depends on the context of the conversation since most people are prone to make sideways glances when they are withholding certain information. Maybe they just don't trust you.

In most cases, you will only make credible inferences when you understand what all the eye movements mean as well and connect them to the context of the conversation. Remember, if you are not sure, the best thing to do is to ask more follow-up questions and analyze more signs.

CHAPTER 4: Chapter 4.
Identification of Personality Types

Researchers examined data that was collected from over 1.5 million people and it was found that there is a minimum of four distinct personality groups: reserved, regular, exemplary, and egocentric. The findings go against the existing paradigms that are present in psychology.

The study used questionnaires with questions, in which volunteers volunteered to respond in exchange for more information about their personalities.

People have tried to sort out personality types since ancient times, but the scientific literature has discovered that this did not make sense.

Personality types were only found in self-help literature and did not find any mention in scientific journals. From the answers to the questionnaires, the specialists pointed out the five basic traits of personality: neuroticism, extraversion, openness to new experiences, sympathy, and conscientiousness. Once the new algorithms were developed, there were four types of personalities emerged.

Regular

Regular people are rich in neuroticism and extraversion, and have low levels of openness to new experiences. Women are usually more prone to fall into this category.

Reserved

The reserved individual is emotionally stable but has no openness or neuroticism. He is not extroverted, but he is pleasant and aware.

Exemplary

Exemplary people score low on neuroticism and high on all other characteristics. There are more women in this category. The likelihood of someone being exemplary increases with age. They are the kind of people that you can trust, and they are open to new ideas. These are the kind of people that will take care of things.

Egocentric

This group scores very extroversion and below the required score in openness, sympathy, and awareness. These are people you do not want to leave. There has been a substantial decrease in self-centered numbers as people age, both with women and men.

Researchers also developed a new method, reducing the possibility of aggregation of the algorithms. This procedure revealed the four groups.

To make sure the categories were accurate, they used a group of egocentrics adolescent boys to validate the information. We know that adolescents behave in an egocentric way. "If the algorithms were correct and selected for demographic data, the results would point to the egocentric as the largest group of people in that situation."

According to experts, this research can help health care professionals evaluate people with extreme personalities. In addition, you can collaborate with the selection of candidates in job vacancies or even for those who are looking for a loving partner.

The analysis also points out that as mature people, their personality types changed. For example, older people are usually a lot more conscientious and sympathetic than people that fall under the age of 20 years. When we look at people in large groups, it becomes very clear that trends exist. Some people can change their characteristics over time.

Classification of Personality Types

The classification of your personality type is by the combination of 4 criteria.

These criteria are the opposite and exclusive. For example, if you are extroverted, you cannot be introverted. For a personality to be formed, it is necessary to choose a criterion of each criterion. In the end, the combination of the four chosen criteria gives the personality type, for example, ENTP or INFJ.

Check out the acronyms and the four classification criteria below:

Introverts or Extroverts

The first classification of personality types is related to the way we interact with the world. Concerning this question, we can be: Extroverts (E) or Introverts (I):

Extroverts (E): Who has this type of personality is extremely sociable and likes to talk and interact with other people. He is not afraid to state his opinions and is very communicative. Focus your energy on the real world.

Introverts (I): These are usually people who feel better alone, are less sociable, and interact with fewer people. In general, they do not open easily. They concentrate their energy on the world of thoughts.

Sensory or Intuitive

The second classification of personality types is related to how we observe and absorb information from the world. Concerning this criterion, we can be: Sensorial (S) or Intuitive (N):

Sensory (S): Corresponds to the most materialistic personality type, obtains information through the observation of facts and concrete details. They are realistic and practical people.

Intuitive (N): These are people who have a more imaginative profile. Instead of obtaining information through concrete facts, they prefer to observe and draw conclusions from their own thoughts and beliefs. They are the most creative and complex people.

Thinkers or Sentimental

The third classification of personality types concerns how we judge other people's actions and also how we make decisions. About this criterion, we can be: Thinkers (T) or Sentimental (F):

Thinkers (T): They make decisions and always judge people based on logic, generally weighing the pros and cons of the situation. They are objective and fair, they rarely let feelings influence their decisions. They value logic, justice, and equality among people.

Sentimental (F): People with this type of personality judge people and make their decisions guided by their instincts and also by feelings (decide based on what they are feeling at the moment). They value harmony, empathy does not follow strict rules, they accept exceptions well.

Judges or Perceptive

The fourth classification of personality types is related to how we prefer to live, whether we prefer to act spontaneously or whether we prefer to think well before acting. For this criterion, we can be: Judges (J) or Perceptive (P):

Judges (J): Whoever has the type of judging personality is satisfied after decisions have been made, they are distressed by letting problems accumulate. In general, do not think much before acting, prefer to regret later.

Perceptive (P): They are more satisfied to make well-thought-out and more accurate decisions; they take time to act. Perceptions become distressed if they need to make a decision quickly. They usually think hard before they act because they are afraid to repent.

CHAPTER 5:

How to Analyze the Truth in a Relationship?

In a one-on-one relationship, it can be difficult to know what is really going on in your partner's mind. You might feel like you are fighting an uphill battle when you try to figure out what your significant other is thinking or feeling at any given moment; and oftentimes, this lack of insight causes arguments or anxiety between the two of you.

It can be hard to know objectively if the relationship is headed in the right direction or not. It's not like you can see a "relationship meter" that will tell you how strong the bond between you is. The fact is, there are no visible cues.

However, to answer the question of whether your combination is ideal and right for each other or not, several questions can help you arrive at an objective answer.

To analyze the truth in a relationship, ask yourself these questions:

1. Is my partner respectfully honest with me? If you have to answer "no" to this question, it doesn't mean that you are involved with an inherently dishonest person. It can mean that you are in a relationship with someone who isn't comfortable enough with themselves to be completely honest with you.
    It could also mean that they are not confident enough to tell you things that might make you upset. As a result, they may be communicating dishonestly without meaning to. However, this doesn't mean that they aren't telling the truth at other times; it just means that they aren't always completely truthful.

2. Does my partner have trouble saying "no" to me? If you have to answer "yes" to this question, it could mean that your significant other is more egotistical than honest. They may feel compelled to please you in every way, but they aren't necessarily honest about it.

   Another possibility is that they lack the self-confidence necessary to say "no" or assert their own opinions confidently. They may be afraid of upsetting you or not want to come off as refusing you in any way.

3. Does my partner persistently lie to me? If you have to answer "yes" to this question, it probably means that the person you are with is not entirely honest with you on a regular basis. If they lied once or twice, they may only be trying to hide something from you that makes them feel bad or uncomfortable about themselves.

   However, if they tell you lie after lie without regret, their dishonesty is likely the result of low self-esteem or insecurity. They are not convinced that you will love them so they have trouble telling you the truth about anything.

4. Does my partner often tell stories that stretch the truth? If you have to answer "yes" to this question, it could mean that their dishonesty is more of a personality quirk than any form of deception. They may have a hard time accepting the limitations in their own abilities, so they will embellish details of situations that they were involved in to make themselves seem more powerful, successful, or brave.

   They may also habitually make up stories about how well they did something based on one simple detail so that it sounds like the situation was much more significant than it was.

5. Is my partner easy to read? If you have to answer "yes" to this question, it probably means that your partner is generally honest with you. The fact that they are insecure or lack confidence in themselves makes them want to come across as honest at all times so that their low self-esteem doesn't stand out in contrast.

However, it's possible that they could have a certain "tell" that reveals when they are feeling nervous about something. For instance, if your partner is telling you a story from work and they are stuttering while doing so, it could be that they aren't confident about telling you the rest of the details. They may not want to upset you by being dishonest, but they also don't feel completely comfortable being honest either.

6. Do I feel like my partner needs me more than I need them? If you have to answer "yes" to this question, it means that there is a significant imbalance of closeness in your relationship. It could mean that your partner does not respect you in the way that you deserve or simply doesn't care about your feelings.

7. It could also mean that they feel as though they can't exist without you at their side and are trying to manipulate you with their dishonesty.

Is dishonesty always focused on small things? If you have to answer "yes" to this question, it means that your partner's dishonesty is often tied to their personality quirk and isn't intentionally meant to manipulate you or hurt your feelings.

CHAPTER 6:

Powerful Techniques for Unmasking People Through Their Body Language

The Mosaic Technique

This technique means that you have to start with one small thing. For example, you wanted to get information about a woman's name. This can be done simply by watching the face and eyes. Then, slowly look at her clothes or hands for details about her life or interests, so you can use it in conversations to keep it going once the conversation is started.

The Head-Tilt Test

Another technique that is used by most people to develop trust is the head tilt test. This is very simple; all you need to do is tilt your head sideways and listen to people's explanations about a particular thing. If they are telling the truth, their voice, as well as body, tends to go down; whereas if they are lying, then their voice goes up. This is because when the body goes up, it means that they are trying to convince themselves.

The Arm-Cross Test

This is another technique used by most people to know whether they are telling the truth or not. This is done by placing one's hand on their chest and another on their stomach. It helps in knowing whether they were telling a lie or not. If they are lying, then their hand feels heavy on the stomach as they tend to be more tensed; whereas, if they are telling the truth, then it feels normal as there is no tension.

The Shoulder Shrug Test

Another technique for reading the body language of people is the shoulder shrug test. It means that when it comes to making a decision, there can be two types of reaction which are very typical. The first one is that they can shrug their shoulders or make a small gesture of confusion. And the second type is that you can see them raising both their shoulders up while thinking about it. This means that they are confused or not sure about the decision which they want to take. People need to be careful while reading body language as wrong analysis can cause a lot of problems in life. People should use their inner intuition before using any of these techniques.

The Leg Tilt Test

It is one of the most effective techniques of body language. The technique is very simple; all you need to do is to stand in front of a person and slightly tilt yourself to get a better view of their legs.

By doing this, you can read some vital signs like sweating, trembling or vibration which can help tell whether he or she was lying or not or are just feeling nervous.

The Micro-Expression Test

It is another technique that is very much helpful in knowing someone's emotions. It means that when a person is talking to you, he or she will be making some movements with eyebrows which can help know whether they are lying or not.

For example: while having a conversation with some people, you can see that their left eyebrow is making a movement which indicates that they are lying.

The Handshake Test

It is another technique that can help know the body language of people. It means that when it comes to shaking hands with someone else, there will be some signs like sweaty palms or it will be too hard or too soft.

All these things will help in knowing the body language of the other person and can help make a better relationship with them.

CHAPTER 7:

Detecting Lies

The science of detecting lies has had some breakthroughs, but it's still hard to tell just by looking at someone whether they are telling the truth. There's a ton of room for detection errors in a formal interview setting.

Not All Lies Are the Same

Liars use several different methods to prevent detection and escape from awkward situations—especially when under pressure or time constraints such as a formal interview. This article will explore those methods.

The Most Important Lie-Detecting Skill Is Viewing the Person Being Interviewed

In order to detect lies, you first need to analyze the person firsthand. This means looking at their facial expressions and observing their body language. You have to be in a position where you can see both the person's face and their hands, or be standing directly in front of them so that you can look them straight in the eyes. The biggest mistake people make is trying to detect a lie through voice analysis, which is next-to-impossible to do accurately. Let's now look at some of the most common methods people use to avoid detection when they lie.

A "Lie" Isn'

One of the biggest mistakes is assuming that all lies come from intentional falsehoods. That's not always true. Sometimes a person might be telling the truth—then remember something that is inconsistent with what they are saying—and from there, forget to correct their statement.

The Most Common Lie-Concealing Method Is Through a "Bypassing Interruption"

This is when someone makes a statement and then immediately changes subjects to avoid direct questions about the original statement. This is done as a way to avoid getting caught in a lie or to conceal the inconsistency in what they are saying.

Why People Usually Don't Use This Method

It is very uncomfortable for untrained people to switch topics mid-sentence. Not only that, but if they become too good at it, it could make them appear suspicious. That's why most liars usually choose to use other methods instead.

How to Disprove a Use of a "Bypassing Interruption"

If you confront the person, insist they finish the original sentence.

The Most Common Lie-Concealing Method Is "Vagueness"

This is when someone makes a statement, but they don't provide enough details to be able to prove it as true or false. This is a very common method of lying.

Why Vagueness Is Used

Sometimes people want to just vaguely leave an impression of something, but don't want the details to be questioned or proven false. This method can also be used as a way to divert attention away from the real message. For example, if someone is trying to describe something that happened at work and comes across as vague and unclear, that might suggest he or she is concealing something about that situation.

How to Disprove Vagueness

When a person is vague about a statement, ask them to specify exactly what happened and to provide specific details. Or you can ask them to explain their statement in greater detail. If they don't do that, that's usually a major sign they are being evasive.

The Most Common Lie-Concealing Method Is "False Hand Signals"

This method is not as common as the others, but it's still a good way to detect lies. People will make up hand gestures or even tell little stories to distract from what they are actually saying. The purpose of this method is to cover up something the person doesn't want you to notice.

Why People Use False Hand Signals

Sometimes a person will unconsciously gesture with their hands while telling a story, usually as a way of distracting you from the truth of their statement. For example, they might gesture left and right with their hands to describe driving around the block. This is done to convey that they drove around the block—but it doesn't mean what it sounds like it means. They might have driven around the block to cut through a side street or alley, which would take them away from their destination.

How to Disprove False Hand Signals

This one is easy. Simply ask the person what they did with their hands that relate to what they were saying. For example, if someone says that they drove around the block, you can ask them to show you how they turned their steering wheel. If their hand gestures don't match up, then it's a lie.

The Most Common Lie-Concealing Method Is "Diversion"

This is when someone makes a statement and immediately changes the subject in an attempt to avoid any questions that might raise suspicion.

Why People Use Diversion

Most times, people use the diversion to divert attention away from something they are hiding. It's usually used as a way to get you off their trail and avoid answering your questions about what they just said.

CHAPTER 8:

Powerful Tips for Reading and Analyzing People

How to Read a Person Like a Book?

Understanding people is one of the greatest skills you can have. It's difficult without practice, but it's not impossible for some coaching and observation. If you find yourself in need of an interpersonal makeover, start by reading these tips for getting to know someone from head-to-toe without saying anything at all.

Trust Your Gut

Look for body language that seems out of place, in contrast to the way they are speaking or who they are talking to. Also, check for inconsistencies in their gestures and clothes. A great example is a person who is dressed very nicely but is crossing their arms at you defensively.

Look for Over-the-Top Displays of Affection

People who are truly impressed with you will not be afraid to show it. If the person is showing awkwardly over-friendly behavior, they might just be trying to get on your good side.

Listen to the Volume

Some people, especially those who are shy or insecure about themselves, will not speak very loudly because they are afraid of being heard. Others, especially those with something to prove or an inflated sense of self-worth, will project their voice to intimidate.

Listen for Restricted Vocabulary

If they're using whole phrases and you notice they keep repeating them over and over, they might be trying to put on a show. They may also use key terms that let you know exactly who exactly you are dealing with.

Track Their Complaints

Their complaints could also be an indication of insecurity or poor self-esteem.

Look for the "N" Word

It can be in their clothing, hairstyle, jewelry, and much more. A great example is the trademark of Nautica apparel. Women typically wear the nameplate on their purse or shoe, while men might wear it on their belts.

Inconsistency

If you notice a sudden behavior change, it could be because they've just come into contact with someone they know who has a conflicting opinion or interest in them. It is usually some sort of business deal or personal matter that will cause them to suddenly change who they are.

Don't Forget About the Hands

When someone is anxious, their hands can give them away by fidgeting and trembling. If they are trying to portray a sense of confidence, they will be much more at ease with their hands.

Watch for the Drink

If they are drinking, you might want to consider either: a) how much they have or b) what it is. Someone who is trying to fit in with a certain crowd might be drinking something obscure, while someone who wants to seem classy will probably be sipping on a fine drink.

Seating Position

People who are confident in themselves and their situation will tend to sit closer together. It may also indicate how they feel about their situation. People who are feeling powerful will be more spread out, while those who feel powerless will usually draw in closer.

Observe for a Talking Partner

If you notice they have a partner or friend sitting with them, do you notice them talking and laughing? If so, the person sitting with them is most likely an influencer of some kind whom they want to impress you with. Don't be fooled, however, because it may also mean the person is nervous and will try to divert your attention to someone else.

The Big Ears

Listen for the word "you." People who are trying to win you over will use it constantly in conversation, while people who feel superior to you will try to emphasize their point without using it much at all.

Watch for Visual Add-Ons

They might be wearing jewelry, accessories, or clothing with an interesting message or meaning behind them. Not only can this show a lot about who they are, but it will also help you to get to know them better.

Observe Size

How do they feel about themselves? Truly confident people will be proud and comfortable in their skin, while people who aren't confident will try to make up for their stature by wearing certain types of clothing or shoes.

CHAPTER 9:

Expert Techniques for Controlling Difficult People

If you are working with difficult people, or you have to live with them, this article is for you. Difficult people can be a devil of a problem. They are not going away as we know, and they may escalate in frequency as we get older. How do we survive these difficult relationships?

These techniques are simple and easy to master. Simultaneously, they are powerful enough to bring about positive change in your relationships with difficult people. After you learn these techniques and use them a few times, you will be delighted with the results. I guarantee it!

The First Answer Is (Start With): Be Nice!

Difficult people often have low impulse control and/or they like to overreact to people who overreact in response to them. You will get far more cooperation from difficult people by being nice. The best way to be nice is to keep your voice low and calm sounding and stay very focused on the task at hand.

If you're dealing with a person who is not well or has some kind of disability, these techniques can work miracles for you. If you have a family member with autism or developmental disabilities and other people in the family are having trouble staying calm, help them by showing them these techniques. You'll be doing them a favor.

The first answer to difficult people is "Be Nice!"

The Second Answer (Which Is Very Important) Is: Don't Take Things Personally!

If you take things personally, you are more likely to overreact in the presence of difficult people. Overreacting leads to a downward spiral of increasing emotional intensity. You may even try to get your own back or get revenge by being difficult to back. You may try to "get even" by being mean or withholding.

Or you may react in a passive-aggressive manner by finding little ways to punish difficult people for their bad behavior or their insensitive words and actions. When you overreact, your relationships suffer! When you take things personally, the relationship problems will increase. Overreacting is a downward spiral that can get out of control very quickly. This leads to bad outcomes in the relationship.

The second answer to difficult people is, "Don't take things personally. Be nice. Stay calm.

"The Third Answer (I Call It the "Parachute Answer") Is: Ignore Them!

If you are dealing with an angry or combative person, and you try being nice, and you try not taking it personally, but the person still won't cooperate with you, then ignore them. Walk away. Go on to other things that are more important than trying to make this difficult person happy. Don't try to win them over. Don't explain yourself or apologize to them. Just ignore them.

Go do something else that makes you feel good, or that yields some kind of reward for the effort involved.

I call this the "parachute answer" because when you are dealing with difficult people, you can ignore them like a skydiver who pulls the ripcord from his parachute. The skydiver floats away to safety and saves himself from a rough landing.

The third answer to difficult people is, "Ignore them."

The Fourth Answer to Difficult People Is: Get Out of the Situation

If you are in a situation with difficult people, and being nice, and not taking it personally doesn't yield cooperation or positive change, then get out of the situation. This is particularly true if you are dealing with a toxic personality disorder or some other kind of mental illness. Get out of the relationship.

If difficult people are not going to change, and this is particularly true if they have a chemical imbalance in their brain or another mental illness, then your efforts to be nice, and to ignore them, and to get on with more important things will be futile. You will need to leave the scene of the crime if you want to save yourself from becoming a casualty.

The fourth answer to difficult people is: "Get out of the situation if the difficult person is not going to change."

The Fifth Answer to Difficult People Is: Become the Change You Want to See!

This strategy only works if you are dealing with a person who has some degree of freedom in the situation. It is not going to work with a person who is locked up in prison, or who has lost custody of their children, or who is dependent on someone else for food and shelter. If you are dealing with a person like this, you can't change them. You can only escape from them.

But if you are dealing with a person who has some freedom to control their behavior and their own words and actions, then you can become the change that will make them want to cooperate with you. This takes skill in handling relationships, of course. You have to know how to be polite and how to give people compliments if you want them to cooperate with you.

The payoff is that it works.

You will still meet with resistance from difficult people, but you can overcome their resistance by using a combination of strategies that I call the "Five Steps to Overcoming Resistance." They are:

Be Nice! Don't take things personally. Be confident and persistent without being aggressive or demanding. Listen carefully without interrupting or arguing. If you need to, use questions and open-ended statements instead of statements that can be answered with a simple "yes" or "no."

CHAPTER 10:

Tricks for Analyzing a Deceiver and Taking Control

There is nothing that one can rely on from the words of a deceiver. It does not matter if they are the emperor or a regular person.

1. The deceiver says they did not do it, and yet there is clear proof that they did it, then you know the truth is different from what they say.
2. The deceiver claims to be innocent, yet they have a great deal of hatred against the person who is accusing them.
3. The deceiver says it is just a misunderstanding, and that they did not do anything wrong.
4. The deceiver writes something to defend their actions in an attempt to clear their name, but they reveal more about their crime than the initial accusation did.
5. The deceiver says they are sorry for the people who were hurt.
6. The deceiver claims to know what their accusers value, and they attack this value to save themselves.
7. The deceiver makes a story about their suffering, but we do not know if that story is true or not.
8. The deceiver uses language to shield themselves from blame instead of taking responsibility for their actions.
9. The deceiver says people should be more forgiving.
10. The deceiver tries to make themselves look good by saying they are not the only one who is guilty of bad behavior, but everyone else does it too.

11. The deceiver makes a list of excuses for why they did something bad, but their excuses contradict each other or do not make sense at all.

12. The deceiver tries to trap their accusers in something they are not saying, which is a turnabout from what they are accused of.

13. The deceiver talks about how they were wronged when it is clear that the actions they took towards others were offensive and hurtful.

14. The deceiver says it was an accident, but there is proof that it was intentional.

15. The deceiver claims to be innocent, but there is no proof that what they say is true.

16. The deceiver blames evil forces for taking over their mind and forcing them to do bad things.

17. The deceiver says they have given up doing something bad, but we will see the same behavior in the future.

18. The deceiver wants to blame someone else for their problem, even though it is not possible to transfer responsibility.

19. The deceiver uses excuses like "I was young" or "I was drunk" when they were old enough and sober enough to know better than to engage in those actions.

20. The deceiver says they are not the only one who has done bad things, but their actions were worse than what others have done.

21. The deceiver says that if they admit to something, then the rest of us will not be safe from attack.

22. The deceiver tries to deny something, even though there is proof that proves they did it.

23. The deceiver wants to make themselves look good, by saying they won't do something bad.

24. The deceiver tries to use a colorful metaphor to hide the truth that they did something bad.

25. The deceiver tries to make us think that they have more power than they have, by boasting about all of their resources and connections.

26. The deceiver says, "you can't prove it" or "you can't prove this happened," even though we know it did happen from other proof we can find.

CHAPTER 11:

Interpreting Body Gestures

There are two ways to deliver a message when you are engaged in a conversation. Of course, the usual way is simply by talking; however, there is another way that is also as effective but is often overlooked, and that is through the use of gestures. Gestures as small acts that you do while you talk. In fact, by learning how to read gestures, it is even possible to say if the person whom you are talking to is lying or not. Gestures may also reveal the current mental and emotional state of a person. As they say, "Actions speak louder than words." Indeed, if you want to master the art of manipulation, then learning how to use, as well as read, gestures are very important.

Take note that a gesture is not limited to the movements of the hand or crossing of the arms. It can also involve such small and often neglected movements with the eyes. If you want to stress something strongly, it is suggested that you say it while looking directly into a person's eyes. Also, leaning slightly forward while placing your hand on your chin and nodding your head would show that you are eagerly listening to the other person as he talks. Snapping your fingers is also often used to show that you have just realized something. As you can see, there are so many gestures that you can do. Gestures add more energy and give more expression, which makes the conversation more interesting.

Learning how to interpret gestures is also important. Again, the key to manipulating a subject is having a good understanding of your subject. Crossing arms and/or legs usually shows a defensive posture. It may show that the other person is not being open and relaxed. Covering one's mouth, as well as touching the ear, may mean that the person is lying. If you want to know what a certain gesture may mean, a good piece of advice is to do the gesture yourself and be open to how it makes you feel.

Of course, there is always the possibility for gestures to be interpreted differently. For example, just because a person rubs his nose as he tells you something does not always mean that he is lying to you. However, although gestures may be hard to decode at times, they will allow you to have a better insight and understanding of a person.

What if the person with whom you are talking does not use gestures? Indeed, you cannot compel someone to express themselves with gestures as they talk. Also, gestures, to be real and authentic, must come naturally. Most of the time, when a person remains calm and still, it is only a sign that you need to do more to penetrate his defenses. Once you can get into his mind, he will be more open than he usually is and will naturally use gestures as he talks to you. To do this, simply make him more relaxed and encourage openness.

CHAPTER 12:

How to Analyze People Based on Their Body Language?

The same way you train a dog to listen to your body language and cues, you can train a human being to follow you without question. The first step to control those around you lies in analyzing them, however, which is why this will discuss how to analyze people based on their body language.

Positive Body Language

There is a chance that you or someone you are observing is feeling insecure and trying to mask it. However, if you are not dealing with the melancholic personality, you might be dealing with a choleric personality. Everyone has heard the phrase "Fake it until you make it." This is the dogma of the choleric personality type. Whether they were cut out for something or not, they will not give up easily.

If you are confronting this type of personality, simply the mere act of uncrossing your arms or legs should gain you a little confidence. Add to that a genuine smile for the next person that you encounter and watch as they lighten up a bit in response. It might take a little practice, but this type of body language gives you control of the situation.

Understanding Eye Contact

This one can be tricky as it is easy to misinterpret, but long eye contact is almost always meaningful in some way, shape, or form. If a person can look at you without looking away for more than a few seconds, then usually they are confident around you and are likely to be genuine. This is likely to be your phlegmatic personality type; one who is displaying a little bit of awkward shyness. They will notice you scanning the room, but do not count on them calling you out on this.

Typically, eye contact can make you look interested and says a lot about the person you are dealing with. If you find yourself being stared at by a person, you are likely dealing with a sanguine personality. This personality type is an observer and tends to be the sincerest of the four. By looking people in the eye, it is their way of proving those qualities.

Depending on the situation, you can look down and away out of shyness. When people are shy, they are deemed innocent. Your phlegmatic personalities are really good at this as well. You want to seem innocent, no matter what your intentions, as the best choice for drawing other people in is to keep them interested. Since you want people to trust you, you have to get close enough to analyze what type of personality you are dealing with. If the other party looks away and down, and then back up at you, take advantage of this opportunity to consider them more closely. This is a sign of vulnerability, which means they trust you, so you are free to do with that trust what you may. This is often a good time to ask them about themselves or offer something personal to break the ice. Compliments are always a good choice, as it is hard to dislike someone who has recently played you a compliment.

Smile

The most important asset anyone has is their smile. A smile is a window to the soul. If you are walking down the street and someone gives you a genuine smile, it can change your day. That is the power you want to carry around with you. This is the gift of most sanguine personality types. They are cheerful on the outside and can easily make people laugh. Faking a smile is hard. The truth of any smile lies in the eyes. Pay careful attention to the lines that form when the cheeks rise as the evidence of a genuine smile forms.

If you ask someone to do something and they decline, smile anyway, they will feel bad for saying no. Depending on their actual reaction, say it again in a different way and a cartoonish voice (humor), and follow up with a serious voice. Ask for the favor again by adding another smile. This is best used in social situations and is to be avoided at work. Unless you are super cool with your co-workers or if you are sure you are dealing with a sanguine personality. If your co-worker or your boss displays a dislike for emotions or seems impatient, you could be dealing with a choleric personality. You will need to make it seem like they are the leaders. You're pushing boundaries, but you don't want anyone to recognize this game. No matter how it ends, do not give too much of a reaction. If you are too happy, it could kill the vibe. The same is true if you are too upset, just smile. You will not be able to change your personality type as the theory is that you were born that way. However, knowing more about yourself, you can control the display, or even master your weaknesses to have influence or get close enough to other people, that you may sincerely analyze them.

Negative Personality Cues

Now that you have a basic understanding of positive body language, let us look at the opportunity to dig into the negative cues often given by different personality types. Sometimes even the most trustworthy and genuine people can give off signals of distress through body cues, so it is important to take them with a grain of salt to avoid being misled.

If you find someone who is trying to discourage you, or they are judging you, their personality is likely phlegmatic if the negativity you are picking up on is coming from someone who is demanding attention or seems phony; you are amidst a sanguine personality type. You want to know the difference and how to respond to either situation to achieve a goal. Whether it is to cheer someone up, so you can enjoy their company, or perhaps you need to get away from someone who would seek to destroy your aura. Either way, practice makes perfect, and observing takes a lot of it.

Personal Space

If someone moves away from you, this is often a sign that they believe you either did something wrong or you represent something negative to them.

This mentality applies to all four personality types. It hurts to feel rejected. Instead of feeling sorry for yourself, move back into their realm if you want to change the vibe.

Body Language and Posture

Posture and general movement might also express a big deal of information. A study on body language has developed considerably since prehistoric days; however, well-known media have concentrated on the over-interpretation of protective postures, arm, and leg crossing. Whereas these non-verbal acts can show thoughts and attitudes, the study indicates that body language is far more restrained and less perfect than formerly believed.

Proxemic

Individuals often refer to the need for personal space, which is as well a vital style of non-verbal communication. The level of space people need and the level of space people tend to perceive as belonging to them are swayed by several factors comprising social models, intellectual potential, situational aspects, personality distinctiveness, and level of knowledge.

For instance, the amount of individual space required when having an informal talk with another person frequently varies from one to four feet. On the contrary, the individual distance required when talking to a group of people is approximately eight to twelve feet.

Eye Gaze

The human eyes play an important role in non-verbal communication and such aspects as staring looking and blinking are considered significant non-verbal acts.

When people meet someone or things that they adore, the pace of blinking goes up and pupils enlarge. On the other hand, staring at another individual may show a variety of emotions comprising hostility, concern, and desirability.

People as well use eye gaze as a way to conclude if someone is being sincere. Usually, fixed eye contact is frequently taken as an indication that someone is telling the reality and is dependable. Deceitful eyes and failure to keep eye contact, on the contrary, are often perceived as a pointer that somebody is dishonest or being misleading.

Haptics

Communicating by use of touch is another essential non-verbal conduct. There have been considerable amounts of study on the significance of touch in childhood and infancy. For instance, a baby raised by a negligent mother experiences a lasting deficit in conduct and social relations. Touch generally might be used to communicate love, awareness, compassion, and other related emotions.

On the other hand, touch is similarly used as a technique to communicate both position and authority.

Researchers have established that high-status persons tend to attack other people's individual space with superior rate and strength than lower-status persons. Gender differences as well play a part in how individuals use touch to bring out the intended meaning.

Appearance

People's preference for color, outfits, hairstyles, and other aspects affecting appearance is as well regarded as a way of non-verbal communication. Research has confirmed that diverse colors might suggest different personal moods. Besides, appearance might also change physiological responses, judgments, and understanding. For instance, just imagine all the restrained decisions people rapidly make about somebody based on their look. These initial impressions are vital, that is why specialists propose that work seekers dress properly for interviews with likely employers.

Researchers have also established that appearance might play a part in how individuals are viewed and even how much money they make. For example, a study carried out on attorneys establishes that attorneys who were perceived as more attractive than their workmates earned practically more than those viewed as less good-looking. Culture is a significant sway in how appearances are viewed. While slenderness tends to be respected in Western cultures, some African cultures associate full-figured people with superior health, prosperity, and social class.

Artifacts

Items and images are as well as tools that might be deployed to communicate non-verbally. On an online discussion, for instance, people might pick an avatar to symbolize their distinctiveness online and to converse information concerning who they are and the things they adore. People frequently spend a huge deal of time creating a particular picture and surrounding themselves with items planned to transmit information regarding the things that are vital to them. Uniforms, for instance, may be applied to transmit a marvelous amount of information regarding an individual. A warrior shall put on fatigues, a police force will dress in uniform, and a physician shall dress in a white lab coat. From a bigger perspective, a simple glance at this attire tells everybody what an individual does as an occupation.

CHAPTER 13:

Breathing

There are different ways you can read someone's body language. It can be read by their leg and arm movements, facial expressions, eye contact, or smiles. Do you realize that how a person breathes has meaning, too?

Emotions and how you breathe are connected. You could read a person's feelings by watching the way they breathe. If emotions change, how they breathe might be affected. See if you can notice breathing patterns in your family, friends, coworkers, or significant other. They may not tell you exactly how they are feeling, and it might depend on certain situations.

Deep Breathing Might Indicate Excitement, Attraction, Anger, Fear, or Love

Deep breathing is the easiest pattern to notice. If somebody suddenly starts to hold their breath, they might be feeling a little scared. If someone takes a deep breath and then shouts, they could be angry. Excited people, who are experiencing shock or are surprised, might suck in a deep breath. They might also take in a deep breath and hold it for a few seconds. If their eyes start to glow, this might indicate that they are surprised or excited. A person might start to breathe deeply if they feel an attraction toward another person. You may notice someone take a deep breath in, suck in their stomach, and push their chest out to try and impress somebody they are attracted to.

Sighing Might Signal Hopelessness, Sadness, or Relief

When you sigh, you are letting out a deep, long breath that you can hear. Somebody might sigh if they are feeling relieved after a struggle has passed. They are thankful that their struggle is over. A sign might show sadness or hopelessness, like somebody who is waiting for a date to show up. It could also show tiredness and disappointment.

Rapid, Heavy Breathing Might Show Fear and Tiredness

You may have just seen a person rob a place, and the police are chasing them. You notice they are breathing very rapidly. This is because their lungs need more oxygen since they are exerting much energy. After all, they are running. Their bodies feel tired, and their lungs are trying their best to keep up. We feel the same effects when we feel scared. This will happen when we experience fear; our lungs need more oxygen, so we begin to breathe faster. You will easily see when somebody has been scared or running by noticing the way they are breathing.

Another interesting fact about breath is that smells can influence breath. Any odors that are tied to emotions can change a person's respiration rate. Several studies have shown that the body will respond to bad and good smells by breathing differently. If you were to smell something rotten, you would end up breathing in a shallow and rapid manner. But, if, instead, you smelled baking bread and roses, your breath would be slow and long. The really interesting part of this is that the breathing rate will change before the brain has ever been able to consciously register if the smell is good or bad.

According to Scientific American, the emotions that we have with smells and scents are extremely associative. We started learning about these different smells in the womb, and then during our lives, our brains learn to refine our views of emotional rewards, pleasures, and threats that are contained within a certain odor. If a person breathes deeply, they feel that something is safe, creating a pleasurable emotional state. This means if you notice a person's breathing rate suddenly changes, let your sense of smell catch up first. It could be that they have gotten a whiff of something they either like or dislike.

The interesting thing is that while we can learn how people feel based on how they are breathing, the way a person breathes can also affect their emotions. In a 2006 study published in Behavior Response & Therapy, they discovered that undergraduates who practiced slow-breathing exercises for 15 minutes had a more positive and balanced emotional response afterward than the group faced with 15 minutes of unfocused worrying and attention.

And it doesn't even have to do with just being calm. A French scientist, Pierre Philippot, asked some participants to identify the pattern of breath that they connected with certain emotions such as sadness and joy. They then asked a separate group of people to breathe in a certain manner, and then they probed their emotions. The results they got were amazing. If the subjects were told to breathe in a particular manner, even if they were unaware of it, they said they felt the feeling associated emotion, apparently, out of nowhere.

I want to share one more way you can use a person's breath to tell how they feel. This is something that you can't readily do, but it is still interesting.

A new idea that is being studied about emotions and breath is that what you exhale also plays a role in emotional response and that the chemically analyzed exhales were able to figure out how the person felts. In an article from Science News, the air's chemical makeup within a soccer stadium varies when people begin cheering, and the same is true in movie theaters. They studied 9,500 people as they watched 16 different films that ranged from rom-coms to horrors, and then they studied the air composition of the room to see if it changed during certain scenes that were rather emotional in one way or the other.

The crazy thing is that it did. In suspenseful moments, there was more CO_2 and isoprenes in the air, which are chemicals associated with muscles' tensing. Every type of emotion came with its chemical makeup.

Facial Microexpressions

Learning to decode facial expressions is similar to having superpowers. The face, with all its expressions, which are called microexpressions, could be a window into their soul. Knowing how to read them could help you to understand a lot about how someone is feeling.

Methods of Non-verbal Analysis

To perform any non-verbal behavior analysis, you have to use techniques that can help you describe the behavior in a way so it can be trusted. The advantages of scientific analysis are:

- To select a person's weaknesses and strengths during normal relations.
- To expose lies by using a combination of facial and verbal expressions.
- To anticipate a person's behavior.
- To identify another person's state of mind and emotions.

It doesn't take long to learn these techniques with an interactive and focused program based on specific exercises.

Scientific Based

The first text written about emotional expressions was written by a French neurologist, Guillaume Benjamin Amand Duchenne de Boulogne. This text was written in 1862 and demonstrated the method of using electrodes on the facial muscles to establish their relationship between the facial muscles' movements and the subsequent emotional expression. To honor him, a true, authentic smile can sometimes be called the Duchenne smile.

Charles Darwin wrote the Expressions of the Emotions in Man and Animals in 1872. In this, he says that emotions are just another evolutionary product and are inherited. Body and facial expressions go hand in hand with emotions and look to be the same in people who live in different parts of the world and other animals and primates. Darwin's studies didn't continue after he died because of the scientific community's hostility toward his theories and him. He was criticized for saying animals have emotions. According to his critics, only humans can feel things. His methods were based on observations rather than science.

This concept of emotional expressions being universal was discovered one more time in the late 1950s. Researchers like Birdwhistell, Izard, Ekman, Ellsworth, and Friesen tried to validate Darwin's theory. They worked together to develop a set of theories, tests, and methods that created the "Facial Expression Program." They believed the origin of emotional expressions and emotional experiences would be a specific number of inherited neurological programs. We know now that there are specific paths for every emotion that causes a facial expression associated with that particular emotion. According to the theory of evolution, emotions have adaptive functions that will let a human react through immediate responses to various stimuli for survival.

There are two groups of non-verbal techniques:

- **Decoding technique:** This interprets and will give meaning to movements.
- **Coding technique:** This describes the body and facial movements.

Facial Expression Techniques

ISFE or Interpretative System of Facial Expressions

Jasna Legisa developed this in the NeuroComScience laboratory in 2013. It is a table of what facial movements mean. It comprises a set of descriptions and tables that order and integrate facial expressions according to the emotions they are related to. This information was taken from existing literature and previous systems about this subject.

Other than secondary and primary emotional expressions, other facial signs get described as regulators, illustrators, and manipulators. According to Ekman, Izard, and Hjorstjo, emotional expressions get grouped into "big families." These "families" include many facial expressions that, even though they mean slightly different things, get united because they receive the same emotional range. Within the "surprise" family, you will have an annoying surprise, face surprise, a real surprise, awe, and many more.

Primary emotional movements get put into three categories:

- The first category includes muscular movements that belong to specific emotions.
- The second category includes movements that might belong to primary emotions.
- The third category includes minor variations of emotions that could be part of many emotional families.

These categorizations make the interpretation and accuracy of the whole analysis.

Mimic Language and Man's Face or the Hjorstjo Method

An anatomy professor at Lund University located in Sweden, Hjorstjo, in 1969, tried to systematically categorize certain facial movements with their meanings into eight emotional families. His handbook reports the decoding and coding of facial expressions, so it is possible to determine the facial muscle contractions either in combination or by themselves.

MAX or Maximally Discriminative Coding System

This system gives meaning to the facial movements instead of just describing them. Izard developed MAX in 1979. Later in 1983, he worked with Hembree and Dougherty to create an advanced version of MAX that was named AFFEX. The created facial configurations are based on regular expressions of emotions like shame, disgust, pain, surprise, happiness, interest, fear, sadness, and anger. Every emotion and expression gets classified.

EMACS or Emotional Facial Action Coding System

Friesen and Ekman worked to describe the expressions of six emotional families: fear, surprise, anger, disgust, sadness, and happiness. Hager has been working at Ekman's laboratory since 1994, studying facial expressions by using an automatic computer to identify their techniques. This database has created the FACSAID or FACS Affect Interpretation Dictionary system.

Hanest

During the same year that the first version of FACS was published, the Hanest Manual was also published. The Hanest Manual was created by Gergerian and Emiane, who are two French scientists. It has the same plan as FACS to describe facial movements.

FACS or Facial Action Coding System

Vincent W. Friesen and Paul Ekman in 1978 introduced FACS or the Facial Action Coding System. In 2002, while working with Hager, they release another version.

BabyFACS or Baby Facial Action Coding System

The same structure that is used for adults can be used for small children and babies. During 1993, Oster looked at babies' facial expressions and changed up the descriptions as needed. These are only descriptive and don't give any meaning to the emotions.

CHAPTER 14:

The Hands

It is important to read gestures in the context of other aspects of body language, we will explore ways of reading gestures. We all talk with our hands often. For some people, the gesturing matches their message well. Some people do not deploy hand gestures while others overuse hand gestures. Most hand gestures are universal. A person that does not use hand gestures may be seen as indifferent. For this reason, the audience may feel that one does not care about what the other is talking about. If your hands are hidden, then the audience will find it difficult to trust you. If one's hands are open and the palms wide enough, then the individual is communicating that he or she is being honest and open.

Furthermore, randomly throwing hands in the air while talking may suggest that one is anxious or panicking. Extreme anger will also make one throw their hands in an uncoordinated manner. For further understanding, take time and watch movie characters quarreling, and you will note that most people being accused of something will throw their hands in the air randomly. It is something that they have little control over because most of the body language happens at the subconscious level of the mind. Randomly throwing hands in the air indicates that one is overwhelmed with emotions or that one has given up defending their position in the argument and has left the argument to the individual that started it.

Additionally, one may point at an object or a person. Pointing as a gesture helps the focus of the speaker and the audience to the focused area. During your school days, you probably saw your teacher point in a particular direction without speaking until the students that were talking had to stop. As such, pointing at particular students drew the attention of the entire class in their direction, making them become the center of attention, and they had to do a quick self-evaluation and stop talking. All these illustrate that body language communicates tone and emotions just as verbal communication.

Furthermore, pointing while wafting the index finger indicates a warning. When one points the index finger at someone and wafts it up and down, then you are denoting a stern warning and judgment to the individual. It is the equivalent of saying, "this is the last warning." Probably your parent or teacher may have a point and waft gesture to signal a warning that what you are doing is wrong and that you should stop. In movie characters, you might have observed that the police or the lead actor uses the index finger to warn someone. The finger signal singles out the individual and reduces the focus to just that one aspect of behavior that the speaker wants the target person to understand.

Relatedly, if one spreads all the fingers and holding them together against those of the opposite hand, indicates strong personal reflection such as when praying or remembering the departed soul. The same gesture can be used when one is focusing the mind during meditation or yoga. The holding of each of your fingers against their peers of the other hand may also indicate feeling humble and thankful for everything. For instance, followers of the Catholic faith frequently use this gesture when praying. The gesture shows humility and thankfulness.

Sometimes one may tap on the head once or continuously. When one taps on the head using a hand or a finger, it indicates the individual is thinking hard or trying hard to recall something. For instance, when speaking and you try to remember what another person said, you might use this gesture. Children often tap their heads once or continuously using one finger or the entire palm to signal attempts to recall something. The gesture is the equivalent of saying, "Come on, what was it?" or "Come on, what was the name again!" and it is a prop to recall hard.

Similarly, a fully raised palm with fingers spread may indicate that one should stop. When stopping the vehicle on the roadside, one raises one of their palms high up, and it is taken as a sign to stop. The same is true in the sporting environment where raising one palm high up commonly communicates that the playing should stop.

If one claps, the palms together may indicate applauding the message or the speaker. When the speaker is done with speaking, the audience may clap their hands together to mark appreciation of the message or both the message and the speaker. However, when the hands are spontaneously and violently clapped, then it is a message that the audience should stop because what they are doing is unethical or irritating. At home, one of your parents probably clapped their hands suddenly and violently to make you stop as well as draw attention to their presence, especially where you were playing loudly around the house.

Relatedly, if one interlocks one hand against those of the other hands and folding them. The application of this gesture indicates that one is attentive but unease at the same time. During an interview, meeting, or a class session, the audience is likely to interlock their fingers and fold them. In a way, the interlocking of the fingers is supposed to offer some form of assurance to the affected person that he or she is safe. One is likely to also use this gesture when he or she is mentioned negatively. Think of how you reacted when you were mentioned among noisemakers or workers having challenges following the rules of the company. Most probably, you interlocked your fingers and folded them.

Additionally, if one is feeling shy or uncertain, the individual is also likely to interlock their fingers and raise the interlocked fingers when speaking. The gesture in this context appears to give some sort of prop for the affected individual, enabling them to navigate the anxiety. The gesture in this context is not just about communicating the physiological status of the affected but as a coping mechanism of sudden anxiety and discomfort of the individual.

Still on body language and focusing on gesture, if one raises both hands behind the head and interlocks the fingers, then it is to act as a cushion for the head. The gesture is used to indicate that one is feeling casual, tired, or simply not tasked by the current conversation. The gesture may also indicate that the individual is feeling tired by the conversation or the activity. Think of how you react when feeling exhausted when talking to a friend or after watching a movie. You probably raised both of your hands behind the head and interlocked the fingers to act as a headrest. In most cases, when one invokes this gesture, then the individual is likely to let the mind allow other thoughts to escape from the current conversation.

Correspondingly, there is the gesture where one lets one of their palms brush down their faces. The gesture is used to signal deeper thinking, processing new contradictory information, or accepting humiliation in front of the audience. The gesture suggests surrender. It indicates yielding to inner thoughts or views from the audience that one may have initially opposed. At one point, the class or your friends cornered a speaker facing the speaker to pause and take a minute to admit that he or she may have overlooked some facts about the issue. Probably the speaker used this gesture to indicate defeat.

On the other hand, to indicate rejection or strong disagreement, both hands with palms wide are waved in an alternating manner to create the letter X. In class, you probably drew the letter X using both hands to indicate that you disagree or reject what is being proposed. For instance, as a kid or as a student, you probably drew letter X to signal rejection that you will not follow instructions when the teacher sarcastically indicated that you should not follow his instructions. The sign also indicates retreat to your inner world to avoid listening or watching what the speaker wants.

CHAPTER 15:

Bust and Shoulders

While many people focus their interest on facial expression when making a judgment, the shoulders also play a certain role when it comes to body language.

Raised Shoulders

Raising your shoulders requires that you lift the whole weight of the arms.

This needs effort so that you hold the arms up for a certain period.

When the other person has hunched up against the shoulders, usually with the arms crossed or tight and holding the body can mean that the person is feeling cold. It might also mean that the person is aloof.

Shoulders Curved Forward

When you realize that the person has curved their shoulders forward, you need to read something along the lines of being defensive.

This usually happens when a person feels threatened.

Shoulders Pushed Back

Pushing the shoulders backward forces the chest to come out, which then exposes the torso.

This can be used as a way to taunt you, showing power.

Shrug

The classic shrug usually means negation, and might be accompanied by other body movements, especially facial expressions.

The movement of the shoulder might not be so much, at times; it might be just a slight raising of the arms that you barely notice.

Shrugging usually indicates a sense of uncertainty or a certain lack of understanding. At times, shrugging might show lying when it is more prolonged. So, you need to understand the context in which the shrug is being used to decide whether the shrug is positive or negative.

The Meaning of the Clothes and Ornaments

Discussions about body language are often biased toward features like genuine smiles, pupil dilation, and crossed arms and legs. Most people ignore the importance of appearance and clothing. How you dress tells someone a lot about you, and your perspective of them. If you are attending an event, your attire tells your audience what you think of the event, or how seriously you take it.

On its own, appearance might not mean much to an audience. However, it sets the tone for everything else you might say. If your appearance contrasts the message that they expect from you, working your way up might be a tall order. If your appearance aligns with the message or theme that the audience expects, your work is relatively easier.

Clothing can project a low authority, high authority, or neutral image of yourself. When dressing, remember you are not doing it for yourself but your audience. You have to consider the demographics and cultural expectations because it affects your message.

In case you are meeting an international audience, it is advisable to consider cultural affiliations when dressing. It helps the audience embrace you better. At the same time, however, you should also ensure you are comfortable in your clothes. It would be pointless for you to go the extra mile only to end up uncomfortable and awkward.

Dressing right also affects your confidence. It empowers you and makes you feel good about yourself. You don't feel out of place, in which case you would be in a hurry to get out of the situation you are in. Spare a few minutes on YouTube and find speeches President Obama delivered to working-class citizens. In most of these speeches, he didn't have a jacket on and had his sleeves rolled up. Without uttering a word, he already conveyed a message to them that he is also working hard like they are. This sways the audience and makes it easier for him to address them.

The color of your clothes might be about what you feel that day or something else in your personal space, but it means a lot to a mature audience. Light colors represent flexibility, openness, fresh ideas, and a loud persona. Dark colors represent precision, calmness, and sophistication. Bright colors represent energy, responsiveness, cheer, and stimulation.

What about the prints on your clothes? Curved lines tell people you are approachable, romantic, graceful, and casual. Straight lines, on the other hand, give a picture of a formal individual, persuasive, strong, and crisp.

Of course, even though these might be true, context is still king.

CHAPTER 16:

Proxemics

Now, imagine that you are standing in front of someone. You can see that they are crossing their arms with hands hidden behind them, their eyes shifting nervously from you to veer off to the left now and then. They shift their weight from foot to foot and struggle to maintain eye contact. Something about the body language of this person makes you uneasy, but you cannot place it. They keep their distance from you, and every time you approach closer, you notice that they are likely to move away.

Body language is good at giving us feelings that tell us to be on edge, offended, or relaxed, but if you do not know what you are reading, you will struggle to understand why you feel that way. It can be difficult to know what someone intends to not put meaning to what they are doing. You can have a general idea of how you want to respond, but it can be incredibly beneficial.

Proxemics refers to the distance between yourself and someone else— it is the usage of space between yourself and the world around you. Naturally, people put varying degrees of space between themselves and others. When you are looking to understand proxemics, the best way to do so is to consider it a judgment of the relationship between yourself and those around you. You can also judge others' relationships based upon the distance they put between each other, both vertical and horizontal.

The Use of Vertical Space

Vertical space is what it sounds like—it is the space relative to your position height-wise. When someone utilizes vertical space, they attempt to make themselves taller or shorter, depending on the context. Those who want to make themselves taller may want to be an authority or otherwise as someone deserving of respect and compliance. They may even use this space when they are trying to look at others who are taller than them—they simply tilt their heads back to look down their nose at the taller person to create the same impact.

When you make yourself smaller, you typically want to be seen as less dominant for some reason. You may be attempting to shrink down to speak to a child to be understood truly, for example, or you may be lowering yourself to make yourself seem more submissive. In particular, people will pull their chins inward when they want to be smaller because they will then be required to look up through their eyelashes at the other person, even if the other person is taller.

The default, eye level, is deemed to be the most respectful—it marks you and the other person as equals, deserving of the same respect and consideration.

The Use of Horizontal Space

In horizontal space, you are looking at how near or far people are to each other. You will use this when you are picking apart the relationships of others. There are four distances used between each other, ranging from intimate distances to public distance.

The Intimate Distance

This refers to being as close as possible to the other person. When you are in this position, you are usually touching without trying or close enough to do so. It is typical for young children and parents, or for lovers that are comfortable being this close to each other. Generally speaking, this zone is only about 18 inches away from you.

The Personal Distance

Slightly further away than the intimate distance, the personal distance covers about 18 inches away up to about 5 feet around you. It is what people are talking about when they say that you are invading their personal bubbles. This zone is usually reserved for those you like or feel comfortable with, such as friends and family members or children who are too old to be within the intimate zone. The closer you can get to the center, the closer your relationship with that other person.

The Social Distance

This is a bit further out. It is the distance you naturally try to maintain with strangers around you or interacting with someone else you do not know. Typically, this is between about 5 and 10 feet. You will use this when you are out and about unless you have no choice otherwise. When you are forced to encroach on this distance, you will most often make it a point to ignore the other person in an attempt to ignore the fact that they are violating those personal boundaries, such as sitting on the bus.

The public distance is even further out. It refers to anything beyond 12 feet and is reserved for instances in which you speak out toward a crowd. You want to be loud enough that everyone in the crowd can speak, so you want to ensure that people are a bit further away from you so they can see and hear you easier. It is reserved for lectures in classrooms, for example, or in performances.

CHAPTER 17:

Beware of Bluffing -
When to Notice That a Person Is Lying

Imagine a world where people say the first thing that comes to mind, a world where you told the truth to everyone you talked with.

For example, let's say you took one look at your boss early in the morning only for you to tell him he looks like a weakling.

What do you think would be the result? Peace or chaos? Before I answer that, here's another scenario most people are quite familiar with: your spouse turns around in front of the mirror and asks, "Does this dress make me look fat?" Even if the dress does make her look fat, I know most men will say something along this line, "No, it doesn't, it's probably the mirror playing tricks on you."

So why do we opt to lie or gloss over some important facts? Well, it is to avoid chaos. As we grow older, we have learned the art of deceit to grease our interactions with others and help us maintain healthy social interactions. We know how much the cold, hard truth hurts sometimes, and it's no wonder research supports the fact that social liars are more popular than those who repeatedly say the truth.

This type of lie is referred to as a white lie since we often know the other person is trying not to hurt our feelings.

So, what about the malicious lies people tell to deliberately deceive others for their personal gain? This is what we are going to focus our attention on. We will take a look at the common clues malicious liars give when they lie or withhold the truth. Before we explore these common deception cues, I want you to understand why it's so important to study deception signals.

You and I deserve to know the truth. Society functions on the ability to trust people's words, that people will choose to abide by their words. If it didn't, society would descend into chaos, relationships would have a very short life, there would be no commerce, and parents and children would not trust each other.

In as much as we will sometimes use the white lie to avoid chaos, society also depends on honesty because we would all suffer in the absence of the truth.

Millions of people paid the price with their lives when Adolf Hitler lied to Neville Chamberlain. When Bill Clinton lied, it destroyed the reputation he had built over the years. When Richard Nixon lied, it nearly broke the steadfast loyalty and confidence of the American citizens in their country. Truth is, undoubtedly, essential in all relations, be it professional or personal.

We are lucky that people speak the truth most of the time, and most of the lies we come across are usually social or white lies. When it comes to crucial matters, we need to assess the truth of what we are told.

It is not always easy finding the truth. For millennia, people had to rely on the use of torture devices to get the truth from those suspected of deception. Today, people have learned how to analyze handwriting and voice and use the polygraph test to know the truth.

Still, even with our advanced techniques, there are a lot of concerns about the accuracy of these methods. You may think you have little chance at succeeding when these modern deception analysis techniques can still fail. Don't be discouraged. With practice, you will become better at reading these deceptions cues.

After all, it is impossible to conceal deception.

Why Lying Is Difficult

Practice makes perfect, and most people have spent a good amount of time practicing and honing their lying skills. We have learned how to lie from an early age, and we've done it so often that we have become good at it.

Despite our perceived skills of deception, we still give off non-verbal cues that betray our innermost emotions to the astute observer.

For instance, people tend to smile less when they lie. This is contrary to the popular misconception that we smile more when we lie.

The difficulty in deception is that the subconscious mind gives contrary signals to our verbal statements. That is why it is so easy to catch someone who's not experienced in deception. On the other hand, actors, politicians, and public figures have learned how to refine their body gestures to the level where it's difficult to catch them in a lie. They tend to restrict their gestures in order not to reveal negative or positive gestures when they lie.

Researchers have discovered that it is easier to lie over the phone or an email. It is also easy to lie when part of your body is obscured by the interviewer or interrogator. It is no surprise that law enforcement agencies place their suspect on a chair in the open in a bid to have an unrestricted view of their body language.

How to Detect Deception

People give off different types of signals that reveal deception. Some of these signals are so subtle that even veteran body language readers might miss out on them if they don't know where to look. Some signals are insignificant unless you study them in clusters before you can get an accurate analysis.

In some cases, you will be looking for signals of lies of omission—looking for the hidden piece of information. Other times, you will be searching for lies of commission—verbal statements or actions that are inconsistent with the rest of the message.

Sometimes you won't have access to these deception clues since you might be communicating with the other person via an email or a phone call.

Variables such as ethnicity, gender, and cultural background can also influence how you detect non-verbal deception cues. Let's examine the major signs of deception in people.

Study the Body Language

Every part of the human body betrays our true feelings. By studying the arms, legs, eyes, nose, and torso, you can effectively deduce if someone is lying.

Liars Will Try to Avoid Eye Contact

When lying, people often avert their eyes in order not to betray their true emotions. They often do everything in their power to avoid looking at you since they think their lies will be uncovered through their eyes.

Conversely, people often give you their full attention and concentration when they tell the truth.

Restricted Body Movement

The arms and feet are great indicators of negative emotions, like deceit. It is easy to detect the gestures created by these body parts.

When someone is lying, they tend to be less expressive with their arms or hands. This means they are conscious about exposing themselves.

Have you ever noticed your arm movements when you are passionate about something? Your arms will wave all around as you try to emphasize your point.

When you notice a person sitting with his legs and arms close to his body, it's a sign that he's keeping something in. Watch out for unnatural hand and arm gestures. People who lie often try to overcome their restricted body gestures by using their gestures to convince us of the honesty of their verbal statements.

Involuntary Cover-Up

When the person's hand goes straight to the face when making a statement or responding to a question, it is a clear sign of deceit. Liars often cover their mouths while speaking as if they don't believe what they are saying.

Watch Out for Contradictions and Consistencies

We will take an in-depth look at the correlations between verbal statements and the accompanying body language.

From obvious contradictions, such as shaking your head from side to side while saying yes, to a subtler form of contradiction, such as a pursed lip, you will learn how to accurately interpret these signals.

You will see that these signs occur both at the conscious and subconscious levels. You will notice when people make a conscious effort to embellish their points through their forced gestures and off-timing.

You will also learn how to read people's initial reaction expressions. This is the initial expression you notice on people's faces before they mask it with other body languages. Even if you can't read the fleeting initial expression, it is usually an indication that someone had something to hide.

Observe the Timing

Timing is everything when detecting deception. For example, if a person's head begins to shake in an affirmative direction before the words come out, then there's a high chance he's telling the truth. But if the person's head shakes after the point is made, it is a sign that the person is trying to demonstrate conviction.

Watch out for the arm and hand movements that demonstrate a point after it's been made. This gesture is an afterthought, and it's the work of a shoddy liar. These arm and hand movements won't only start late but also seem mechanical and at war with the "verbal" statement. Someone who is truly convicted about his statement will nod or shake the head in tune with every point he makes. Be aware that a mechanical nodding when there's no point to emphasize is a sign of deception.

Sniff Out the Contradictions

Timing is crucial, but we need to pay more attention to contradictions between verbal and non-verbal cues. The woman who smiles while saying, "I hate you" is sending a contradictory signal. There's an obvious disharmony between her facial expression and verbal statement. Another example is a man telling his girlfriend or spouse he loves her while clenching his fists. Similarly, the gesture and the verbal statement are not in harmony.

Study the Timing of the Emotion

It is also difficult to fake the timing of emotions. For you to detect deception, carefully observe the timing of the emotions, and you will never be fooled. A fake emotion is not spontaneous; there's usually a delay in the onset of the emotion. The fake emotion lasts longer than normal and ends abruptly. Let's take the emotion of surprise to paint this point. The surprise emotion is always fleeting, and it is a fake response if it lasts too long. So, when people feign surprise, they usually keep the surprised face longer than usual.

The Unhappy Smile

Here's another contradiction you need to watch out for. I briefly touched on this aspect when I explained the concept of smiles. I elaborated on the difference between fake and real smiles and how the former is limited to only the mouth area. When you pay close attention, you will notice that most deception signals are restricted to the mouth region.

Interpersonal Interactions

You need to consider a lot of factors when searching for signs of deception in people. Take a look at their posture concerning the environment. Observe their stance to see if it's defensive or offensive. Research shows that guilty people are likely to go on the defensive since they feel they are boxed in. So, let's examine the types of cues you will get from someone who's on the defensive.

CHAPTER 18:

Non-Verbal Signs

As social creatures, we have a long history of utilizing sure non-verbal signs to show interest in others or check whether others are keen on us.

Today, with our cutting-edge conduct, this has become more refined, however sure antiquated signs are still there and can be utilized with excellent outcomes. Enchantment isn't restricted to drawing in the other gender or a similar sex contingent upon your sexual direction. The craft of magic is tied in with getting others pulled into you, so you have more power over your relationship with them. The temptation is a forced game played at all levels. A man might need to entice a lady to take her to bed. A lady should attract a rich man so she can have a peaceful monetary life. A vocalist might need to allure the majority with her appeal so she can sell her music. A legislator might need to entice the electors to get to the workplace.

The temptation is to convince, to ruin, or "to lead-off track." Enticement can be both negative and positive. Decidedly, it very well may be tied in with beguiling somebody, causing somebody to have a positive outlook on themselves, or decreasing their pointless feelings of trepidation. Adversely, it may be utilizing impulse to mislead individuals and get them to accomplish something that they wouldn't ordinarily do.

In this part, you will discover a progression of non-verbal communication rules that positively help you utilize the craft of temptation to get what you need.

Cause to Notice Yourself

Drop something and afterward twist down to get it. Models are a glove, a book, a watch, or a napkin

Individuals are customized to see development. When you take this action, others will see your growth and are bound to focus on you.

Mirror Your Partner

Mirror each move the individual you are attempting to tempt makes. At the point when he folds his legs, duplicate it. In the end, when he lifts his hands behind his head, repeat it. If he contacts his face, do likewise.

How Can It Work?

At the point when you and the individual you are communicating with move-in synchronize and match each other's non-verbal communication, you suggest that you think the equivalent. The other individual will get this non-verbal sign unwittingly and may feel that he is genuinely alright with you toward the experience's finish. As a rule, we discover individuals who resemble us more appealing. Reflecting can be tempting, as it tends to be oblivious.

Seem Vulnerable

- **Female**
    - o Show the rear of your wrist.
    - o Tilt your neck and uncover it.
- **Male and Female**
    - o Wear a shirt with an open neckline and contact your neck or collarbone.

The neck and the rear of the wrist are weak pieces of the body. By indicating these parts undefended to an individual, you suggest that you believe them and are not apprehensive. An inadequate non-verbal communication likewise infers you may be happy to go above and beyond with other worthless pieces of the body.

Be Visible More Than Others

- Walk near the individual that you need to tempt.
- Aim to be inside their field of view more regularly than others.
- Bump into them a few times with the goal that you become a recognizable face.
- Make a casual discussion about breaking the ice, so you presently don't feel like outsiders.

If others see you frequently, they are bound to get inspired by you. Commonality prompts interest. Plan to be around an objective individual more regularly than others. In time, they will undoubtedly give more consideration to you than others.

For instance, trying to say hey to an individual you don't know on various events will, at last, make you a natural face. It will be much simpler to interface with them, become more amicable, and take it to the following level. Keep in mind that you can't be enchanting on the off chance you are not taken note of. The non-verbal communication of an enticer consistently expects to stand out.

Seem Approachable

For Ladies

Tilt your head down and turn upward with your eyes. A side tilt now and again joins this.

This exemplary signal emulates how a kid may admire a parent. Because of stature contrast, a youngster will consistently gaze upward with wide eyes. It is a motion that proposes blamelessness and is generally utilized by young ladies.

As a grown-up, you can utilize a comparative signal to show accommodation to an expected accomplice and demonstrate that you can be drawn nearer.

Contacting a Person

- Touch an individual's shoulder.
- Touch an individual's hand.
- Hold an individual's hand.

You can begin with an incidental touch on the off chance you need to allure an individual to become acquainted with them. This can be a light touch on the hand while trading something or sitting intently together. It will serve to break the ice with regards to contact. Specifically, this can be your beginning stage while alluring a lady. This non-verbal communication strategy is especially appropriate to those from nations that are socially more hesitant to contact.

When all is said in done, contact can be very ground-breaking. Examination shows that servers who make a light touch while conveying a bill for their clients are bound to get a bigger tip. Curiously, the client is uninformed of the communication and just "feels" like tipping more when the opportunity arrives. The astute server then trades it in for spendable dough by discovering a touch more about non-verbal communication.

In another examination, if a clerk in a retail shop gently contacts a client's hand, when the client is paying for a product, the client will probably rate the exchange and the experience more emphatically than if the client was not contacted. Once more, this is enrolled on an oblivious level.

Appear Exotic

- Surprise individuals by how you look.
- Appear offbeat and intriguing, promising experience.
- Look not quite the same as the common and exhausting.
- Present yourself at first with a vital service.

This procedure is maybe best depicted by the activities of the expert of temptation. It was year 48 B.C. what's more, Julius Caesar was in an Egyptian castle having a gathering with his military commanders. A gatekeeper announced that a Greek vendor needed to meet the Roman general to introduce a significant blessing. Caesar permitted the trader to approach. The trader came in conveying an enormous moved-up floor covering. Once before Caesar, the shipper fixed the rope tied around the floor covering and spread out the rug with a fast snap of his wrist. In this way, revealing a youthful wonderful half-bare woman, the young Cleopatra, the sovereign of Egypt, covered up inside the carpet!

It got everybody off guard, Caesar, as it was evident how much Cleopatra had gone to design this move, getting carried into the city with the assurance of just one man to pull off this trick. The move was enchanting to such an extent that Caesar was snared. For the following four years, Cleopatra proceeded with her expound tempting game, totally charming him.

Like Cleopatra, plan your passage, what you look like, and your general non-verbal communication to recommend that you give an essential experience.

Be Symmetrical
Non-verbal Sign

- Use cosmetics to show up as balanced as could reasonably be expected. It is especially pertinent to ladies.
- Wear evenly lovely material.

Analysts have discovered a connection between evenness and sexual choice. We will, in general, be pulled into individuals who have even faces and bodies. The development gives a coherent response to this. The individuals who are ill-suited or unfortunate will, in general, have topsy-turvy bodies. Henceforth, any deviation from evenness shows that a specific individual has not developed appropriately or is unsuitable for multiplication. It prompts sexual determination where an even individual is viewed as more appealing. Facial evenness is utilized as a pointer of well-being and consequently is viewed as appealing. If your utilization of cosmetics or fabric makes you look balanced, you are bound to seem alluring. Beginning with an incredible impression when initially acquainted with somebody can make the resulting experience much more straightforward. Furthermore, when individuals know nothing about you, they will be anxious to discover more about you, so they can cause an unpleasant estimation of where you have a place. It is safe to say that you are a genuine possibility? What class of society do you have a home with? Is it true that you merit managing? It is safe to say that you are a companion or an adversary? It is safe to say that you are rich or poor? Is it accurate to say that you are in to sell or say you are in to purchase? Would there be a present moment or long-haul advantage in interfacing with you?

Usually, to precisely respond to these inquiries, it takes significantly more than an initial introduction. We as a whole plan to appraise a response for these inquiries dependent on what we see and experience inside an initial couple of moments of seeing somebody. It is completed predominantly with non-verbal communication and non-verbal signs, alongside the underlying short welcome and conceivable casual discussion. Fortunately, you are your promoter. You can prepare for the experience. You can handle precisely how you need to show up, what to state, how to communicate by motions, and how to be seen. With such a significant amount of rivalry in publicizing and catching individuals' consideration, getting the initial introductions right is critical.

Be Prepared for First Impressions

When going to meet somebody unexpectedly, regardless of whether it is for business or delight, you should ensure that you show up at your best. The exact opposite thing you need is to be rushed, fail to remember something, or look ill-equipped. If you seem ill-equipped, the other individual's impression of you is that of an individual who doesn't generally think about that experience or them. It is unquestionable, not a decent beginning. Your most significant point is to improve your early introduction and to show the other individual that you care about them and their necessities.

We should repeat over that once more. The initial introduction isn't about you. It is about the impression the other individual sees about you. Henceforth, it is eventually about them; it is tied in with causing them to feel that you will help their lives and tackle a portion of their issues or improve a part of their lives. In any case, individuals would have a minimal motivator to cooperate with you by any means.

Focusing on this fundamental objective, you can utilize the accompanying non-verbal communication rules:

- Dress appropriately, and such that makes the other individual agreeable when you are near.
- Be on schedule with the goal that the other individual realizes you are energetic and care about his time.
- Appear sure and ingenious, so the other individual understands that he is managing somebody worth his time.
- Be loose and open with the goal that you can like this cause the other individual to feel loose.

CHAPTER 19:

What Really Motivate Us?

Now, we're going to talk about the motivations of people. It's the principal thing that keeps them going and if you want to be able to read a person's body language correctly, you need to be able to understand the motivations that drive them towards that end goal. Think of this as driving on a highway. Every person is driving towards a destination, which is their main motivation. If you're driving right alongside them, you might not be 100% sure of where they're going. However, if you take a good look at the car's movements, the blinkers, the position on the lane, and so on, you should be able to make a close-to-accurate prediction and therefore adjust your own driving accordingly. Even if a person lies to you, knowing what motivates them or what their "end game" is can help you figure out what the lie is all about.

This one is going to be a little more difficult, so bear with me as we go through this. One more note, motives are defined as the conscious or unconscious moving factors for people's behaviors. These motives are the reasons we do what we do. Behaviors are the performances themselves or the actions that are reflective of a person's motivation.

Maslow's Hierarchy of Needs

This is possibly one of the oldest rationales for understanding human motivation. It's not perfect, but what is? Maslow's Hierarchy of Needs is a lot like the Nutrition Pyramid. It explains that motives have a bottom-up approach. The bottom needs are the most basic and prevalent, which must be met first before the others' needs are addressed. There are five levels to basic human need, starting from the bottom, and these are Physiological, Safety, Love/Belonging, Esteem, and Self-Actualization.

Here is a brief look at how this works:

Physiological Needs

These are the main components that are aimed towards survival. According to Maslow's theory, humans are compelled to fulfill these needs first before they can ascend to higher levels. So, what exactly are these physiological needs? These are:

Homeostasis, or the balance of the body to preserve its living condition:

- Health
- Food
- Water
- Sleep
- Clothes
- Shelter
- Social Belonging

Once you have the most basic needs and security, the next step is to seek out social belonging. We are social animals after all, and the need to be accepted by our peers is one of the most common driving forces for people. The need for social belonging is typically met by the following:

- Friendships
- Intimacy
- Family

The need to be accepted in social groups is true regardless of the size of the group itself. This is why even when a person forms part of a small club in school, they still need to be part of the social circle within that club. Small social connections include family, friends, and colleagues in the typical workforce. You will notice that most people will go to extra lengths to have this sense of acceptance and belongingness in their chosen social circle. Failure to meet these needs leads to problems like social anxiety, clinical depression, and loneliness.

Self-Esteem

Fourth is self-esteem, which is somehow connected to the third level. One thing you'll notice is that most people use the third level to jump to the fourth. Acceptance in their social circle tends to promote a person's self-esteem as they find themselves worthy because others find them worthy. What does this level cover? There are two versions of this: the lower and the higher version. The higher version speaks of self-esteem derived from others. There's a need for status, fame, prestige, recognition, and attention from others. This is the one I was mentioning before.

The more difficult version is the higher one which speaks of self-esteem deriving from your competency. This speaks of self-confidence, of knowing that you're capable of independence. This means being able to take care of yourself, know your needs, and have the ability to meet those needs. This gives an individual a sense of value and prevents the possibility of having an inferiority complex.

Self-Actualization

This is the toughest level of the motivation pyramid and is all about managing to reach a person's full potential. Maslow describes it as the ability of an individual to accomplish everything they can achieve in life. It is a lifetime goal and for many people, it can be difficult to pinpoint that lifetime goal. Others, however, know what this goal is but have a hard time reaching the lower levels.

Self-actualization can include:

- Parenting
- Partner acquisition
- Utilizing and developing abilities
- Utilizing and developing talents
- Pursuing other goals

These self-actualization motives are described by Maslow as the intrinsic drive that pushes people forward into completion. People who have a clear grasp of this goal need to understand how their four needs in the pyramid interact with each other to help them achieve the ultimate goal.

Transcendence

Oddly enough, the developer of this hierarchy has also talked about a sixth level. He called it Transcendence and according to him; it is a level of achievement where a person surrenders himself to something or someone more powerful than himself. You are probably thinking about religion, but that's not all there is to it. Transcendence is also pursued through meditative exercises. According to him, transcendence refers to the highest and most holistic level of human consciousness.

So How Does This Help with Reading People?

If we rely completely on Maslow's Hierarchy of Needs, you'll note that most people's actions are built towards reaching any of these five needs. It can be a tad difficult, but what you want to do is try to figure which of these five needs a person wants to achieve when confronted with a particular behavior. Do they want social acceptance? Do they want to achieve the necessities of maintaining life? Or do they want to have a sense of security? If you can figure out exactly what ultimate need one wants to fulfill, you can at least fill in the gaps between and make a reading on what their body is saying.

Experience Matters When It Comes to Motives

There is a lot more to motivation than just figuring out which of the five needs a person wants to meet. The fact is that experience is a big predictor when it comes to figuring out motivations. Plus, it's on a case-by-case basis, with YOU as a big factor in the equation. Simply put— what does this person want from me? What need is this person trying to fulfill through me? What need can I fill for this person?

Guidelines for Understanding People

Let's say you're ready to figure out people's motivations and understand them to forge better connections. The question now is this: how do you start? The way you start varies from person to person, but there are certain "general rules" that can help you move forward with connections.

Here are some of the typical guidelines to make things easier for you:

Most Social Behaviors Are Hidden

We've been talking about the different actions of people and what they mean, but it's also important to look at the opposite end of the scale. You should keep in mind that more often than not; people draw in instead of pushing out. Many actions or reactions are done to suppress rather than express. For example, people close their arms, suck in their lips, or look away from people. It's a pull motion rather than a push. How does this apply when you're trying to connect with people?

Well now, you have to pay extra attention. There's this precious moment between a push and a pull when a person starts to react about something and then quickly holds that back in because they realize that they're showing emotions and feelings they don't want people to see. That's the moment you have to watch out for looking at people.

Now, you might not always catch this deliberate inaction but, knowing that they're there, is half the battle. More importantly, this should tell you that a lot of things are beneath the surface. This is why you need to focus on empathy, delving deep into the surface instead of just interpreting what people say without applying empathy. Put yourself in the person's shoes and you should be able to at least have an idea of what they're trying to do or what they're trying to achieve.

Conceit Trumps Malice

Another thing to keep in mind is that people aren't naturally evil. If you're going to guess a person's motivation, malice should NOT be your first choice. In law, accused people are often considered "innocent until proven guilty" because the default setting is that a person is "good" unless there's enough evidence to show that they've been bad. This is also important if you want to understand people better.

In any situation where people are doing something harmful to others, first, assume that they're doing it because they're unaware or ignorant, or believe that their way is more important. By having this mindset, you are more likely to react more kindly. Chances are you'd react by explaining to them exactly why their choice of action is not the best one. In contrast, walking into a situation believing a person is simply "evil" makes you react badly, perhaps even rudely or even violently.

Selfish Altruism Often Dictates Behavior

Selfishness is often viewed as a desire to please only yourself, while altruism is its exact opposite. Altruistic people are said to be selfless or want only the best for others. Oddly enough, people are driven by these two factors at the same time. Perhaps the simplest way to explain this is: people are giving, but they are giving in a way that also helps themselves. For example, people have no problem lending money to a friend, knowing that this particular friend can help them fix their computer or fix their car without charge. You trade in a car from a dealer and the two of you benefit.

In some cases, helping someone is a sign that you have more power than that person, therefore helping you establish a feeling of dominance over another person.

Memory Is Fickle

Another thing that might help you in understanding people for the better is that they don't have excellent memories. Memory is incredibly fickle for people, and people are likely to forget certain things, ideas, or concepts. Hence, if you're expecting someone to call or someone promised to do something for you, you can always assume it's because they simply forgot instead of deliberate malice. Do not go this route and assume that people are naturally evil as this will leave you feeling bitter and closed to the possibility of connecting and understanding others. You can also make this memory work in your favor. This is because when it comes to connecting with others, people are more likely to remember you if there are similarities as opposed to dissimilarities.

CHAPTER 20:

Practical Application

How does it feel to have a solid understanding of how to improve your communication style right now for better results? How does it feel to know with continued practice, you can master any social interaction and get what you want?

You have mastered this class. Now, implement it in your life. The more you practice the techniques and principles you've learned, the easier it becomes to do it. Soon, reading the silent broadcasts of others will be as easy as reading a name tag.

Are there areas of your circumstance you'd like to improve? Pay attention to your broadcasting and how you can alter it. Whether it's your posture or your eye contact, you have the information you need to make a deliberate broadcast. Practice how you'd like your broadcast to go to yourself in the mirror or on camera. Select a couple of persuasive techniques you'd like to try. Think of a good place to test them out and put yourself there to test them. Don't stop at just testing them out. This isn't an offhand application. The art of analyzing others and using emotional intelligence is a highly structured and formulaic application of communication.

What You Can Do for Better Results

Follow these tips and tricks below, and with regular practice, you can be the most composed, and most compelling individual in the room.

Keep a hand-written or even cloud-based journal of your results each time you set out to test. Consider what you want the outcome to be, and how close you get to that goal. It will be equally beneficial to record details like your environment, mood, and the broadcast of the people in your environment, other influences, unplanned events, and so forth. While this sounds like a bit of effort, it pays off. The patterns that become visible to you are useful information that can be used for your end goal. Some of these exercises will resonate with you more strongly than others. Stick to the ones you like and don't force yourself to engage in exercises that feel uncomfortable or stressed, as these may only increase feelings of self-doubt or wrong-doing. Some exercises may sound too simple or silly for you, but you're encouraged to give each exercise and technique a chance. It's not unusual to find that the simplest concepts are the trickiest; the silliest seeming practices may be the most revealing.

Humans Are Creatures of Habit

Rather than try to break that, you aim to use it. Set a time to meditate each day. Make it approximately the same time each day, too, so that that body physiologically learns the new and healthy patterns you're implementing.

Take Time at the Moment

Some of these exercises will require you to be in an unhealthy or negative idea forming before you can use the techniques. In addition to setting aside specific times to practice, include spontaneous practice. Use a few exercises or techniques that require no preparation, special location, or specific materials for your spontaneous practice.

Be Patient with Yourself

You've been trained very well to over-analyze and self-criticize, so it will take a little practice before you start to dissolve those patterns and establish new ones. Being patient, gentle, and forgiving with yourself in this process will teach you to be the same way with yourself in future endeavors.

Be Patient with Others

Others may not be as ready and as open as you to understanding this and making positive changes. That's okay. It's not your job to make them ready, and it's not your job to teach them. Your focus is on your behaviors and your practice and the improvement of deliberate communication. If others are interested in the changes you're making, it may feel comfortable and nice to share this information with them and listen to the information they have about these ideas. When others aren't interested or are made uncomfortable, don't force it.

Don't Stop Here

This is only the beginning. This information has primed you to go into the world and discover the world of positive and deliberate influence.

Exercises and Practice for Masterful Analysis of Others and Broadcasting of Yourself

You'll find several basic exercises to practice enhancing your analysis of others and influence social interaction with deliberate communication. Select one or two you're comfortable with and start there. When you've become comfortable with those, select one or two more, and even add other practices you've found elsewhere and learned by observing others. Learning from others, you admire and then mirroring that behavior is an effective process of adapting a more influential behavior. The key is to practice them regularly and to record your results.

Regulate Your Breath

This is a common breathing technique used in meditation and the practice of mindfulness. Like most breathing exercises, this is designed to guide the individual into a slower frame of mind that most often includes a slowing and calming of the body, as well. The individual is encouraged to listen to, and focus on, their breath. When the mind wanders, gently guide it back to the breathing exercise.

This exercise can be practiced almost anywhere and at most times, but it does require the individual to block out the rest of the world for a solid 5–10 minutes for maximum benefit. There is no preparation necessary, and while it's nice to practice this exercise in a comfortable and relaxing space, it's possible to implement this in a space that isn't perfect. Doing so will only strengthen your resilience to block out distractions and concentrate deliberately for 5–10 minutes.

The primary function of this exercise is to regulate a slow and steady breathing pattern of 3-count inhales, and 5-count exhales. It's also suggested that when breathing in, you breathe deeply through your nose, and when exhaling, you do so through the mouth as if you're blowing air out from your lips.

By adding this breathing exercise to your repertoire, you'll improve focus and memory and decrease stress chemicals in the body. This exercise also decreases the overall sense of anxiety, lowers heart rate and blood pressure, relieves muscle tension, and improves eyesight.

To practice this exercise:

Get as comfortable and quiet as possible where you can sit undisturbed for 5–10 minutes.

Sit comfortably and close your eyes.

Breathe in deeply as you normally would and exhale.

Hold your breathing for a moment on the exhale.

Inhale again, but this time, breathe in slowly and steadily for a count of 3 in your head.

Hold your breath for a count of 3 in your head.

Exhale, but this time, exhale slowly and steadily for a count of 5 in your head.

Inhale again, slowly and steadily for a 3-count.

Exhale again, slowly and steadily for a 5-count.

Continue this pattern of slow and steady inhales and exhales at a 3-count, and 5-count, respectively.

You may opt to continue to hold your breath in between inhaling and exhaling as part of your pattern, but it's not mandatory. Do that which is most comfortable. If the mind begins to wander, gently bring it back to the observation of the breathing process. Your analytical mind should be listening closely to your breathing for any sign of faster or unsteady flow. The analytical mind can also remain focused on the evenness of your counts, trying to maintain the slow and steady flow. After a 5- or 10-minute period, you can slowly open your eyes and readjust to your immediate surroundings. With regular practice of this breathing exercise, you will teach your mind and body that you have the power to bring yourself to this peaceful moment whenever you want. This is a personal micro-vacation you can use any time in your day; it feels good.

Try Reframing

In reframing, you're encouraged to take a situation you feel negatively about, and put it in a new light; paint a different picture about it. This can be done anywhere, at any time, and takes only seconds or minutes. It can be done silently in your mind, or out loud. Reframing out loud has the added benefit of strengthening the story, and the emotion of the story, to the subconscious mind with an additional auditory version of the story.

This exercise works well for individuals who regularly overthink, and form exaggerated and dramatic stories based on one small piece of evidence, often taken out of context. Examples of situations that reframing can work well on might be someone standing you up for a date, someone taking the seat you saved, someone cutting you off in the grocery aisle, a stranger giving you a nasty look, and so on. These situations often put us on the defensive quickly, as we feel we're wrongly judged or mistreated. It's easy to imagine a personal injustice or that the situation was done against you.

To reduce this pattern of negative thoughts, and to practice positive thoughts, this exercise forces the individual to look at the situation objectively as if no personal emotion was involved. Through this lens, the individual can often slow the pattern of negative thought and put the situation into a more realistic perspective.

There are no step-by-step instructions for this practice. When you notice a situation, you feel personally offended by, stop. Take a moment to analyze what's going on from an objective point of view. Ask yourself if you could be seeing some of these details wrong and if something else, which is not a personal attack on you, could be going on. Imagine a scenario in your mind, where the same situation plays out, but it has nothing to do with you. For example, the person who stood you up could have had an emergency. The person who took your seat probably didn't realize they did it. The person who cuts you off in the grocery aisle could have been in an important rush to get somewhere. The stranger with the nasty look could have made that face because of a thought of their own, and they just happened to be facing your direction.

Read Others in Public

The next time you're in any line, make a point to take your time reading and observing the body language of others around you; both customers and clerks. Note the correlations you observe, and even make notes on your phone about this while you're in line. Take time about once a month or once a quarter to look back over that which you've recorded to analyze your progress and the spots you still may need more work.

Exercise Written Influence

In-person interactions are a prime way to maximize influence, but this isn't always possible. Many times, we interact with others on the phone, in chat, or on social media. If email and text are the way you communicate for most of the day, try writing a persuasive email at least once per day. Plan what outcome you want to see and then try to implement one or two of these tactics to see if you can get the email recipient to do what you want or agree with you.

CHAPTER 21:

How to Fake Your Body Language?

Now, we will go through some easy and simple ways to fake your body language to come across as different emotions or expressions to those around you. These methods can be beneficial in everyday life as well as in the workplace. They can also serve you well in starting out relationships for the first time. These methods also do a good job of helping you feel how you are trying to feel. Have you ever heard the cliché, "fake it till you make it?" Well, in some ways, this is true. By pretending to feel a lot of the emotions, you may be able to convince yourself that you feel that way.

1. Taking a Deep Breath

By amplifying the supply of oxygen within our lungs, we can be given more power and more ability to fake our emotions through body language. This will also give us a moment to collect our composure and pretend to be calm and collected. Also, deep breathing tends to stimulate the parasympathetic nervous system, which can trigger a relaxation response. This is very good, especially when trying to trick those around you into believing that you are calm and controlled in a situation. Deep breathing is a very good trick for mindful living, as it gives you more control over your body and your reactions to stimuli.

2. Controlling the Movement of Our Eyebrows

Our eyebrows can convey a lot about our inner feelings. A lot of movement from our eyebrows can convey feelings that you do not want to express.

You need to consciously be aware of the movement of your eyebrows when you are trying to fake certain emotions through your body language.

3. Trying Not to Use a Fake Smile

While it is good to smile, even if you don't feel like it, that is not always beneficial when faking your emotions through body language. While looking happy and bubbly may make others want to like you, it is not the best look to have constantly.

Fake smiles are far too easy to see through, and humans are naturally inclined to try and search for any inconsistencies within somebody's smile. A better way to hide your emotions is to keep your mouth straight and not smiling or sad.

4. Relaxing Your Face

By keeping your facial muscles relaxed, you can more easily control the movements of your face. Stay away from movements such as teeth grinding, frowning, or displaying any other type of emotional expression.

Having relaxation and a calmer look on your face makes it easier to control better the emotions you are putting out through your body language.

5. Supporting Your Head

A person's head that is being held up by an individual or a face buried into one's palm is a very obvious and clear giveaway of a bad mood or sadness. It is better to keep your head held up high and your neck and back straight in a situation where you feel sad, but you do not want those around you to know that you feel sad.

6. Avoiding Fidgeting

Moving suddenly or very quickly are obvious signs of discomfort and anxiety. If you try to relax your body and try to look as though you are comfortable where you are, then it can be easier to control your emotions and feelings. It also becomes harder for those around you to decipher what you feel because you simply look calm and relaxed.

7. Speaking in a Balanced Tone

This one is very important. If you want to come across as anything other than how you are currently feeling, you may want to take a moment to think about what you're going to say and speak in a balanced and even tone to those around you. The tone of your voice can give away your thoughts faster than you could think. Speaking too fast or changing your tone very quickly and frequently is an obvious sign that you aren't quite sure what you are trying to emote or what you are feeling. Try to slow down before you answer any questions. In addition to this, try to speak with your mind in a logical setting. You will want to focus exclusively on facts and remove any emotion from the situation. Through focusing on facts, you can stop your body from exclusively feeling the said emotions and focus on the task at hand.

8. Trying to Disassociate

If you can manage to detach yourself from a situation you are in, it will become much easier to control your body language and the emotions that you were putting off. An easy way to do this is to think of happy thoughts as good memories. Doing this will help you take your mind off of whatever is happening around you, and it will make it more challenging for others to read your thoughts. By detaching yourself from the situation around you, you will more easily be able to see the logical side of what is happening and able to accurately portray the particular body language and emotions that you want to exude.

9. Speaking to Yourself

You will be able to tell your mind to think about the way that it should. This will make it easier to control your body language and your emotions, as you are in the process of controlling your mind.

CHAPTER 22:

Dark Psychology

What Do We Mean By Dark Psychology?

At its root, dark psychology is all about mind control. You can influence what other people think or do by understanding the inner workings of the other person's mind. You can persuade them into behaving in specific ways, making them feel as though what they have done is of their own volition even though you were behind the scenes, orchestrating the actions the entire time.

You can motivate people to help you by helping them first. You know that they are more likely to offer help if you allow them first simply because people tend to reciprocate. When you understand how the minds of those around you work, you can begin utilizing it to your advantage.

Uses of Dark Psychology

Dark psychology is used widely throughout a wide range of scenarios, some of which are more sinister, while others are typically seen as far less harmful.

Each of the following groups utilizes concepts included in dark psychology to get desired results: Religion, politics, cults, terrorist organizations, abusers, and salespeople all rely heavily on the ideas of dark psychology, pulling strings behind the backs of other people to get what they want.

Usually, when an individual goes out of their way to victimize or manipulate someone else, the drive behind such actions is money, vengeance, sex, love, or power. This type of behavior can be easily understood, as most of us can relate to such emotions. But there are those whose motivation does not come from any of those driving factors. They hurt, kill, and manipulate people just because. This inherent darkness or evil, as some would term such actions, is present in the psyche of every human being, whether in times past or our modern society. There are no exceptions. This nature, latent or manifested to cause harm to those who have done us no wrong, is a very complex study indeed, but one which must be undertaken for the continuous flourishing of society.

If left unchecked, the growing population of predators, arsonists, serial killers, thieves, and other forms of violent and harmful behaviors would become too much of a problem to then be controlled.

Many would object to the generalization that contained in them are such propensities for purposeless evil. Yet, even those fleeting dark thoughts would say otherwise. For many of us, these grotesque images and thoughts of ways to undo another person for no particular reason do not stay in our minds very long, and we cringe when they cross our conscious thoughts or when we act, however briefly, in their direction. But, whether full-blown or short-lived, these thoughts and actions are proof that we all are capable of some degree of 'evil.'

Within the study of dark psychology, some terms arise which should be understood. They include dark singularity, dark continuum, and dark factor.

Primarily used between nations, it can also be employed in a variety of situations such as battles, insurgencies, or riots. In practice, modern methods may also involve the use of communications technology to disseminate pre-prepared messages to mass populations.

CHAPTER 23:

The Dark Traits and the Dark Triad

Introduction to the Infamous Dark Triad

What is the Dark Triad?

The dark triad is a commonly used psychological term used to refer to narcissism, Machiavellianism, and psychopathy. Still, in the dark, Psychology, the actions triggered by these traits can have both positive and negative results.

These traits, though characteristically distinct, tend to overlap in the individuals who possess them. Thus they're often referred to together. A psychopath, for example, may have narcissistic traits. Or someone who engages in Machiavellian actions may also be a narcissist.

Think of the dark triad as a three-part overlapping Venn diagram. An individual can lay in one section, two sections, or even all sections. The more of the dark triad an individual possesses, the more dangerous and difficult it is to detect. Those whose personalities fall within the dark triad might be more likely to commit crimes, cause purposeful societal disorganization, and cause political unrest. At the same time, narcissists, psychopaths, and Machiavellians are also expected to be more charismatic, making it also that much more likely that they would be at the forefront of said crime rings, social hierarchies, or political organizations.

Dark Traits

Machiavellianism

A person with the Machiavellianism trait will possess and exhibit some or many of the following tendencies:

- Focus on their interests and ambitions.
- Give high priority to money and power above relationships Perceived by others as both charming and confident.
- Tend to exploit and manipulate other people to get ahead.
- Tell lies and are deceitful when they think it is required.
- Are prone to flattery.
- Lack of values and principles.
- Appear to be aloof, or very hard to get to know.
- Are cynical of any form of goodness and morality.
- Will easily cause harm to others to enable them to achieve their means.

Narcissism

When a person is in a narcissist's life, they tend to go along with them instead of having to face their coldness and rage. The following are the symptoms of narcissism:

- A grandiose sense of self-importance/self-worth.
- Live in a world of fantasy that supports their delusions of grandeur.
- Are in a constant quest for praise and admiration.
- Have an exaggerated sense of entitlement.
- Often demeans, bullies, belittles, and intimidates other people.

Psychopathy

The 'Hare Psychopathy Checklist; Revised' is commonly used to identify psychopaths. This checklist identifies and makes use of the following symptoms and signs of psychopathy:

- A grandiose sense of self-worth.
- A constant craving for stimulation.
- Superficial charm and glibness.
- Being a pathological liar.
- Being cunning and manipulative.
- Absolute lack of remorse or guilt.
- Absence of empathy exhibited by callousness.
- Lack of deep emotions.
- Living a parasitic lifestyle by using other people.
- Lack of control over one's behavior.
- Sexual promiscuity.
- Early signs of behavioral problems.
- Absence of realistic long-term goals.
- Easily acts on impulse.
- Irresponsible behavior.
- Blaming others for one's faults and not accepting responsibility.
- Having several marital relationships.
- Delinquency at a young age.
- Tends to revoke a conditional release.
- Criminal tendencies/acts in several areas of life (criminally versatile).
- It could be targeted at keeping a relationship from breaking off.

CHAPTER 24:

What Is Persuasion

What Is Persuasion

Persuasion is an honest way of taking control of the thinking and behavior of the intended victim. Aristotle gave four reasons why everyone should learn the art of persuasion:

1. Justice and truth are perfect; thus, the speaker is at fault if the case is lost.
2. It is the best way to teach.
3. An excellent rhetorician can argue both sides to understand the problem and all options fully.
4. Nothing better you can use to defend yourself.

Aspects of Persuasion

The Greeks started the art of persuasion led by Aristotle. In the old days, trials were held in an Assembly, and judgment depended on either the defense or prosecutor's persuasiveness. Speakers were trained in rhetoric and elocution. Greek Philosopher Aristotle defines rhetoric as "a combination of the science of logic and an ethical branch of politics" following his three persuasive elements: Logos, Pathos and Ethos.

Logos

Logos appeals to logic, reasons, and words in your arguments. Logos employs facts, historical and literal analogies, statistics, citing experts and authorities on the subject of debate. In Logos, your words, reasons, statistics, naming, and analogies are like pieces of the jigsaw puzzle that you can put together to construct a logical argument. Your succeeding opinion should not contradict your first argument, but instead, re-affirm and support your first argument.

Ethos

Ethos appeals to ethics. You need to establish your credibility and character; everything you say is right, and you are not just spouting lies. Developing this by how you speak, what language to use, sound unbiased, using right grammar and syntax, and choosing proper vocabulary. Learning elocution is the right way of developing ethos. Your pedigree and accomplishments are essential factors to consider, and you can introduce that without sounding boastful.

Pathos

The third element appeals to emotions. In pathos, invoking the sympathy of your audience is the most crucial part. You can inspire anger or draw pity from your audience through pathos. Develop pathos by using an emotional tone, through expressive language, sharing stories and examples that evoke emotions, and implied meanings.

Many lawyers employ these three elements to win over an argument. If they have mastered these three elements, they can easily win against their opponent.

How to Tell If You Are Persuasive

There will be many situations where you need to think of someone else on the fly. You will not always have the opportunity to research each person, case, or offer to ensure that you know how to sell it in the right way.

Rather than trying to force the case and saying all the right things, you can practice the art of persuading and leading. This technique enables you to lead the conversation subliminally so that you can learn as you go, allowing you to make up your pitch and sell on the spot.

To persuade someone, you want to focus on asking them questions about the specific offer you have. Do not start out asking about the proposal itself.

Instead, ask questions that will help you better understand how and why the proposal suits that person's needs. For example, if you are selling a new software for their computer, ask them how they use their computer and what types of experiences they enjoy most when browsing the internet. Build insight into what they are looking for, then offer them some direction. Once they take it, build further insight into what they need, then provide more guidance. Continue persuading and leading the conversation in this way until you reach the point where you are ready to make your offer. In this way, you are an effective persuader.

CHAPTER 25:

Persuasion vs. Manipulation

Manipulation vs. Persuasion

Manipulation is the dark side of persuasion. We aren't going to tell you how to be manipulative because that's not going to do the world any good. You might be able to get what you want, but you would hurt people along the way. Nothing worth something substantial is going to be gained by taking from other people first. If you wish for long-lasting influence, you have to start to acquire ways to be more of a positively persuasive person.

Don't persuade individuals who aren't going to be able to know any better. If someone isn't knowledgeable and genuinely has trouble understanding basic concepts, it's not fair to manipulate them. You should only help inspire others to think the things they would be able to on their own, just with a little guidance. To inspire someone is to give them a good idea that influences their thinking patterns. It doesn't involve planting an idea in their head and tricking them into thinking something they wouldn't ever have considered on their own.

Never persuade someone to do something that you wouldn't do yourself if they are in the same situation. If you aren't willing to do it, then it's a safe bet that it's not morally right to expect someone else to do it either.

Persuasion should not involve you taking from the other person. It would help if you didn't take something from them that leaves them with nothing. If you do endure from them, you should give them something of equal or more excellent value in the process. It is a shared experience that helps both of you become better people in the end.

There should always be a sense of freedom felt by the other person. Think of it like you would if you were to find a lightning bug in a glass jar. You could put a lid on the pot and keep that lightning bug for your enjoyment. Or you could help the bug and set it free. If you keep it in the jar, it will eventually die, but it will go wherever it pleases if you put it free in the world. You can still help people by giving them their freedom to make decisions that are best for themselves.

First, let's look at the frequent lies and deceptive tactics that you should avoid using at all costs and some other reminders of how you might have been manipulated in the past. So, let's delve into this fascinating and useful subject, shall we?

Get a Good Read on Someone

You want to get to know the person very well. Listen to everything he tells you and glean his speech for potential emotional weapons to use against him.

Anything he confides in you or accidentally reveals to you can be turned into a weapon at any time. Save these weapons in your back pocket for when you need to use them.

What are the best emotional weapons? Guilt is probably the most powerful one of all. People hate feeling guilty. So, find out things that he feels guilty about.

Also, find out things that he loves or cherishes. You can give him these things to make him happy and reward him for his work for you. Or you can cripple him by destroying these things. Love and passion give people power and a will to live. Taking these things away can crush a person. Try to become the gatekeeper of the things that he loves so that you can gain ultimate power over him. For example, bar his access to his loved ones and pitch a fit when he talks to people that you don't approve of, but let him talk to the people he loves whenever he does what you want.

Play the Victim

First of all, you want to believe that you are the victim. You can accomplish this by rationalizing things. Use your conscious processes to justify your actions. Think of ways that others have wronged you to excuse your actions. As long as you believe that you are the victim, then you won't feel guilty about playing the victim card.

You also want to establish your innocence and vulnerability. You want to appear like an innocent victim being harmed by life so that others feel sorry for you. Tell people sob stories about how the world is against you. Make sure that your situations are not self-imposed so that others don't get irritated and think that you just blame others for your problems. A good example of this is talking about how you were abused as a child so that you can explain why you have difficulties picking good love partners and healthy friends now. This excuses your actions and makes you seem like a victim who cannot control his mind or help himself. Strike sympathy in others so that people want to support you. When your subject does anything that you don't like, play the victim card. Show him how deeply he has hurt you. You won't accomplish this by pouting, giving him the silent treatment, or throwing a wild tantrum. You will enjoy way more success playing the victim card if you appear mature and calm about something. Inform him in a steady voice that he has hurt you. Offer him consequences for his actions that he won't like. Say that you feel the need to protect your heart and your interests from him. Also, make him feel like a monster by continuing to appear like a saint who never does any wrong. You don't want to do something wrong to him that he can use as a weapon against you when you play the victim card.

CHAPTER 26:

Dark Persuasion Techniques

Create a Need

This is one of the most fruitful ways of getting a person to change their perspective or way of life. The person trying to persuade a target will either modify a need or capitalize on a market that the subject already has. If this is done correctly, it has the potential of appealing a great deal to the target.

This means that to be successful, the persuader must appeal to the needs that are of more importance to the target. This may be their need to fulfill their dreams or boosting their self-esteem. It may also be their want for love, shelter, or food.

This method will always work out well because there is no way the subject is not going to need any of these things, or in need of anything at all for that matter. Since there is no way the target isn't going to have dreams and aspirations, the persuader will only have to find ways to make the victim understand how they can quickly help them achieve those dreams.

The persuader may also tell their target that the target will realize their dreams if they make specific alterations to their beliefs or perspective. Doing this, according to the persuader, will give the target a higher chance of achieving success.

Appealing to Social Needs

The other technique that the persuader can use is identifying the target's social needs. While this may not yield as many results and the target's primary needs will, it is still an essential tool in the persuader's hands.

Some people are naturally drawn to crowds and desire to be wanted.

They always want to have specific items, not because they need them, but because it comes with a certain prestige that makes them feel like they belong to a higher class.

The notion of appealing to the target's social needs is obtainable through many TV commercials where viewers are encouraged to buy a product not to be "left behind."

When they can identify and appeal to the target's social needs, the result is they can reach a new area of the target's interest.

Making Use of Loaded Words and Images

When a person is trying to persuade someone else, they must be careful with their choice of words, as words can make all the difference. While there are many ways to say a thing, one way of saying it may be more potent than the other.

When it has to do with persuasion, one of the most important things is knowing how to say the right something at the right time. Words are always essential tools in communication and learning the right call-to-action words.

Dark persuasion is one of the most powerful dark psychology concepts, but sadly it is always overlooked and underestimated. This may be because, unlike the other methods of mind control, persuasion leaves the target with a choice. In the other mind control methods, the target is forced into submission, and sometimes this is done by putting them in isolation so that at the end, they do not have any say in the outcome of the process.

When it comes to persuasion, the chips are laid bare (although with an ulterior motive in dark influence) so that the target is left to make the decision that they think will suit them best.

CHAPTER 27:

Brainwashing

What Is Brainwashing

Through the media and motion pictures are seen numerous individuals consider mentally conditioning to be an insidious practice that is finished by the individuals attempting to degenerate, impact, and pick up power. Some who genuinely put stock in the intensity of mentally conditioning accept that individuals surrounding them are trying to control their brains and their conduct.

Generally, the way toward mental conditioning happens in a substantially more unpretentious manner and does not include the vast majority of partner's vile practices. This section will provide significantly more insight into what mental conditioning is and how it can impact its perspective. What is cognitive training? Mentally conditioning in this manual will be talked about as far as its utilization in brain science. In this connection, mental conditioning is alluded to as a technique for idea change through social impact.

This sort of social impact is happening all for the day to each individual, paying little heed to whether they understand it or not. Social impact is the accumulation of techniques utilized to change other individuals' practices, convictions, and frames of mind.

For instance, the working environment's consistency techniques could be viewed as mentally conditioning since they expect you to act and think a particular way when you are in employment.

Mentally programming can turn out to be all the more a social issue in its most extreme structure because these methodologies work at changing how somebody supposes without the subject consenting to it.

How It Works

Many steps go along with the brainwashing process. One of the main requirements that comes with brainwashing being successful is that the subject should be kept in isolation.

The subject can be around other people and affect them, they will find out how to think as a person, and the brainwashing will not work.

When the subject is in isolation, they will go through a process meant to break down themselves. After months of going through all this, the issue will feel like they are wrong, and the guilt will overwhelm them if desired. The subject will be led to think that the new options are all their own and more likely to stick.

The entire process of brainwashing can take some months to even years. It is not going to happen in merely a conversation, and for some parts, it will not be able to occur beyond jail camps and a couple of separated cases. For some features, those who undergo brainwashing have done so when someone is merely attempting to convince them of a new perspective. If you argue with a friend and encourage you that their concepts make sense, you have technically gone through brainwashing. Sure, it might not be wicked, and you were able to think of it all realistically, but you were still convinced to change the beliefs that you held previously. Unusually, someone goes through real brainwashing where they will have their whole value system replaced. It will generally take place during the process of coming around to a new viewpoint, regardless of whether the techniques used were persuasive or not.

Techniques Involved In Brainwashing

Now that we know where brainwashing started, let's look at the definition of the term. Brainwashing can be defined as a process where a person or a group of people use some underhand methods to talk someone into changing their will to that of the manipulator. When discussing this topic, it is important to delineate between honest persuasion and brainwashing. There are several ways that people persuade one another these days, especially in the field of politics.

Here are some of the most common manipulation techniques that you should watch out for:

Isolation

When trying to brainwash a person, one of the first things usually done is the victim's isolation from their family, friends, and loved ones. This ensures that the victim will not have any other person to talk to besides the manipulator. So, the victim will get all their ideas and information from the manipulator while avoiding any possibility of a third party stepping in to ask what is going on.

Attack on the Victim's Self-Esteem

Since the manipulator has successfully isolated the victim, he must look for a way to break his will and self-esteem. They will then use the process to begin to rebuild the victim in whatever image they wish to. The only way a person can be brainwashed is if the person manipulating them is superior to them.

This attack on the person's self-esteem would manifest in intimidation, ridicule, or mocking the victim.

Mental Abuse

The manipulator will try to brainwash their victim by putting them through a phase of mental torture. They will do this by telling lies to the victim and making them feel embarrassed by telling them the truth in front of other people. They can also bully these victims by badgering them and not leaving room for them to have any form of personal space.

Physical Abuse

Manipulators understand many physical techniques can be used to brainwash the victim. These techniques include depriving the victim of sleep and making sure that they stay cold, hungry, or causing bodily harm by exhibiting violent behavior towards them. The manipulator can also make use of some much subtler ways, like increasing the noise levels, making sure that there is a light that is always flickering on and off, or raising or lowering the room's temperature.

Playing Repetitive Music

According to a study, if a person plays a beat repeatedly, especially a moment with a range of about 45 to 72 seconds each minute, it is possible to introduce an incredibly hypnotic state. This is because repetition is much closer to the rhythm that comes from the beat of the heart of a human being. However, this rhythm can cause an alteration to the consciousness of the person until they reach what is known as the Alpha state, which is where the person becomes 25 times more suggestible than he would ordinarily be when they are in a Beta state.

Allowing the Victim to Have Contact with Other Brainwashed People

When the manipulator is brainwashing a person, they ensure that the victim does not encounter any other person/people besides those that are already brainwashed. This is to create room for peer pressure. The truth is that everyone desires to be liked and accepted. This is more prevalent when a person is a new member of a group. In such a case, the person will typically adhere to and promote things that the other members say, which will secure them a space with their new company.

Us vs. Them

This also has to do with the possibility of being accepted by a group. The manipulator makes the victim feel like there is an "us" and a "them." So, they are offering the victim a chance to choose the group they wish to belong to.

This is done to gain absolute loyalty and obedience from the victim.

Love Bombing

This technique has to do with attracting the victim to the group through physical touch and sharing some intimate thoughts with the victim.

Emotional bonding is also used in this technique through a show of excessive affection and constant validation.

All the above mentioned are a few ways to brainwash a person. Once a person is brainwashed, it is usually tough to get them back to normal.

They develop more rigid neural pathways than other people, which could indicate why it is always challenging for a brainwashed person to double-check their situation by rethinking it once they have been brainwashed.

CHAPTER 28:

Deception

What Is Deception

Deception is not usually an easy theme to understand since it involves many different things; for example, distractions, propaganda, camouflage, and concealment. The manipulator is often able to easily control the subject's mind since the victim is often led to placing immense trust in this particular manipulative individual. The victims often believe in whatever the manipulator will say and might even be basing plans and shaping their world base on the things that the manipulator is feeding their subconscious mind. This vital element of trust towards the manipulator can quickly fade away once the victim realizes what is going on. Because of this very reason, a certain level of skill is needed for deployment of this theme, since only then will a manipulator be able to skillfully change the focus of suspicion towards him and onto the victim's paranoia.

In most cases, deception will often present itself in relationship settings and can lead the victim to have dominant feelings of distrust and betrayal between future partners in a relationship. This usually happens because deception is a theme that violates most of the rules of relationships, together with having a negative influence on the expectations that come with the connection. When getting into relationships, one of the things that are usually expected is the ease of having an honest and truthful conversation with a partner.

Types of Deception

As this the case, there are five main types of deceptive tactics that exist. We shall briefly touch on each one to better understand this theme.

Concealments

Probably taking home the medal of most used type of deception, concealment is basically when the deceptive individual knowingly omits information from his often relevant and vital stories to the context. They can also engage in certain behaviors that would signal to hide relevant information from the subject at that particular time. A skilled manipulator is experienced enough to know that he will have to be smart and not direct in their approach, but rather insinuate the lie leading the victim to their conclusion, which is predetermined.

Exaggeration

What can be said about this? This is where an individual, in a sense, stretches the truth a bit too much with an intended goal of leading the story towards a direction that best caters to their needs. The manipulator will make a specific scenario appear to be more severe than avoiding lying directly to their victims. This is usually done to let the victim do whatever it is they want.

Lies

This is one tactic that we, as humans, use daily for one reason or another. We are often inclined to lie as a way to avoid some form of penalty.

For example, if you work in a bank and you are running late because of something minor, you will be inclined to lie to your boss to keep him from cutting you lose. What then can be said for the meaning of this? This is where an individual gives information that is all south of the actual truth.

They will present this completely fabricated truth to the victim, and they will believe it.

Equivocations

This is where an individual will knowingly make a statement of a contra dictionary nature intended to lead the victim to the path of confusion on what exactly seems to be going on. This is usually a smart tactic that will allow the manipulator to save his image if he is later discovered.

Understatements

This is where an individual minimizes aspects of the truth in a particular story being told at the time. They will often approach a victim preaching how something isn't that big of a deal when, in fact, it is of the utmost importance.

CHAPTER 29:

Detecting Deception

If you are interested in knowing the right defense methods against deception, then the first thing you should do is have a clear conscience that allows you to detect fraud as its being deployed. It may be challenging to determine whether deception is occurring or not. Of course, this is unless the manipulator becomes a bit sloppy in his approach and leaves fine breadcrumbs showing that he is indeed languor or offers contradiction of statements. As much as it may be difficult for a manipulator to deceive his victim for an extended period, it is something that we practice on those closest to us daily. What makes detecting deception a bit hard is that no solid indicators are 100% reliable to tell when fraud has happened.

However, deception is capable of placing an enormous burden on the manipulator's cognitive functioning, as they will have to figure out how to recall the agent's functioning. They will also have to figure out how to identify all the statements they made to the subject to keep the story credible and consistent. One slip up and the issue can see something is wrong. Due to the strain of keeping the story straight, the agent is much more likely to leak information that will tip the subject through either non-verbal or verbal indications. Over time, researchers have given us sufficient reason to believe that detecting an attempt of deception is usually a process that is cognitive, fluid, and complex. These processes are not generally constant, as they will often vary, depending on the message that is being relayed. The interpersonal deception theory describes deception to be an iterative and dynamic process of influence between the manipulator, whose sole purpose of this is working towards twisting information to a version that best suits them but is different from the truth, and the victim who will then attempt to figure out if the message being relayed to them is precise or quite the contrary. During this particular exchange, the victim is going to bring to light all the non-verbal and verbal information that will cue the victim into the deceit. At some point in this process, the victim may tell that they are being lied to by the manipulator.

Defenses Against Deception

To avoid falling victim to manipulators, you have to build your defenses to prepare for any manipulative strategies that they may try to use on you. The best way to make your defenses is by taking steps to improve your self-esteem and your willpower. However, as a point of caution, you should be very careful about building your forts because you don't want to create restrictions that will keep you from living a fulfilled life.

For example, as you try to guard against manipulation, you can't act out of fear. You can't hide from the world to avoid scenarios where someone might want to take advantage of you. Remember that the world is full of people with dark personality traits who may harbor malicious intentions, so acting out of fear won't protect you from anyone. It will just make you more of a target. As you build your defenses, make sure that you start on the premise that you are willing to confront manipulators head-on, and you will never run away or recoil. If you act out of fear, you lose by default.

The steps to raise self-esteem: To help you build your defenses, we will discuss the eight steps that you have to take to boost your self-esteem and to increase your willpower by extension.

Acceptance

Acceptance is about assenting to the reality of a given situation. It's about recognizing that a specific condition or process is what it is, even if high levels of discomfort and negativity characterize it.

It's about consciously submitting that something cannot be changed and that its reality is not subject to interpretation. It's about making peace with the situation that you are in.

Acceptance is the opposite of denial. Even the most rational among us tend to be in denial about lots of things in their lives, which are settled facts in the real sense. Rejection can be a coping mechanism that can keep us from being overwhelmed by a given situation's reality. However, denial does us more harm than good because unless we can accept something, we can't change it. We will be stuck looking for alternative interpretations and explanations for our prevailing circumstances.

Detach with Love

Detaching with love is a defense against manipulation that is most commonly used by people who have loved ones who suffer from substance abuse problems. Even though it was conceptualized to help people deal with addicts, you can also work when dealing with manipulators.

Detaching with love is about showing love and compassion for others without taking responsibility for their actions. For example, if you have a family member who is a drug addict, the way it works is to try to support them and encourage them to get clean, but you let them make their own decisions, and you let them suffer the consequences of their actions. If the addict doesn't come home, you don't waste your time looking for them in the seedy parts of the city; you stay at home, do the things that benefit you, and make you happy.

To risk falling into someone's deceptive trap, researchers have come up with some enlightened skepticism questions that can help you to defend yourself against deception. Some of the questions to ask include:

1. What are the things I know about the person's truthfulness?

2. Is the person's statement consistent with the truth or reality?

3. Is there a way to verify or check the authenticity of the statement?

4. What do I stand to gain if I accept and act on the statement?

5. And if I don't gain, what would I lose if I accept and act on the statement?

6. What is the gain of the speaker if I buy into the statement?

7. Is there any part of the statement exaggerated or downplayed by the speaker?

8. Does the idea seem or sound too good to be true?

9. Would I advise my close relation to accept the statement without an iota of doubt?

10. What doesn't feel right?

These 10 questions make you more objective and allow you to think critically when receiving information. When you ask and answer these questions, there is a lesser chance that you will be fooled since you will come across as sincere and sharp, and this will ward off deceivers as they will move on in search of easier targets.

CHAPTER 30:

The Barnum Effect

Whether it's a job interview, a TV show, or a romantic date, subjecting the person of your interest in a line of tedious pre-fabricated questions will bore them out quickly. We all hate answering direct questions about our character, and when asked to 'Name 5 of your worst qualities,' we can even get angry with the interviewer. How is it even their business? It's a very effective way to end your warm and humane relationship with someone, to give them a blank to fill, bore them to tears, and then intrude into their personal space in such an aggressive manner.

Wouldn't it be better to open our functional analysis by letting the person in question know we understand them, identify with them, see what they are, and appreciate them? How then do we open our conversation, and what do we say to break the ice and predispose the person to us instantly?

Here we must resort to a trick used by fortune-tellers and mediums. The scheme may give you a hint of why horoscopes and Tarot readings seem to work, even though they don't make sense scientifically.

This trick is called a 'Barnum effect,' also known as the 'Forer effect,' named after in honor of a famous showman, Phineas Barnum, the first registered user of the so-called 'Barnum statements,' which he employed to 'telepathically read' his audience members or after an American psychologist Bertram Forer, who analyzed the psychological mechanisms behind the said 'telepathy' and recreated the situation experimentally. What he did was offer each of his students a 'unique personality evaluation chart.' consisting entirely of the statements which seem personal but apply to pretty much anyone.

One of the reasons why the Barnum effect works, besides the generalized statements, is confirmation bias. It claims that we tend to agree with our characters' descriptions if we like them, not because they are correct. Maybe you do show a need for admiration; you could be needy and even narcissistic for all we know! And yet, who would disagree with someone calling them reserved, confident, a strong and silent type? It takes individual courage and objectivity, colliding with a good thing said about ourselves, so naturally, we tend to agree.

However, where is the analysis? What we were speaking about until now is related to establishing contact, breaking the ice. What good is someone who answers "Yes" to a Barnum statement?

The analysis begins when we continue the discourse and narrow things down; zoom in on certain qualities of the subject's character that interest us. This technique is called cold reading ('cold' means you're honestly unfamiliar with your topic), and it's used just as often by salesmen, show businessmen, journalists, and scammers.

It helps you study your subject while pretending to know it well from the start. This way, the conversation is much warmer. You can regulate the warmth by interchanging ego-pleasing confirmation-biased remarks, then offering critical judgment in a reasonable and 'sobering' manner, finding essential new information about the subject.

CHAPTER 31:

Mirroring

Mirroring another person should not seem like a problematic notion. It involves the act of mimicking somebody else's body language cues.

While conversing with people, please pay attention to establish whether they mirror one's behavior. For example, at a dinner table, monitor if a person is imitating what you are doing, such as resting their elbow on the table after you or taking a sip out of their glass almost at the same time you did; this indicates that a person is trying to mimic one's body language. An individual who attempts to imitate one's body language helps build a reliable rapport with them. To confirm that a person wants to establish a connection with another, they should change their posture and wait to see if the other person will reposition their posture to match theirs. In a nutshell, they are mirroring attempts to imitate what others are doing, thus, building a strong relationship with them.

Imagine a scenario in which the individual with whom you are conversing is the person who is mirroring you. For this situation, you need to see whether s/he is doing it purposely or not. On the off chance that s/he isn't doing it purposefully, at that point it is an indication that you are now in a state of harmony with him/her. This implies that you would now be able to continue to the following stage of control and apply different strategies that you know. However, if s/he is doing it purposefully, which implies that s/he additionally expects to control you and does it as such, deliberately, at that moment nothing good can come out from such a meeting. The explanation is that no two controllers can match each other, basically because no one in their correct psyche needs to be intentionally controlled.

In such cases, the best thing for you to do is avoid the other individual.

Another thing you can do is basically create a shared arrangement where you can take advantage of each other.

Mirroring is precarious, and conscious work on it, equivalent to the location of the endeavors of individuals to reflect you, takes practice. Consider it as a sonar/producer of sorts, an instinctive gadget typically created more in females than males. You get some feeling from your subject, some impression. Communicate it back by imagining you're them, at that point analyze their reaction. If you need, you could explicitly cause them to depict you as you act like them, to reveal to you their assessment of their character worn as a veil and introduced back to them.

On the off chance that you identify cognizant endeavors to reflect you or copy you, at that point chances are the individual you're speaking with has a place with the alleged dull tern ion: a narcissist, a sociopath, or a Machiavellian type (manipulative). These sorts of individuals use mirroring and psychological sympathy to seduce you and profess to be fundamentally the same as, or a nearby individual to you in a manner you won't have the option to grasp, in an attractive, fascinating way. This bond will give them enthusiastic authority over you since such individuals are not really near you at all by any means. They will frequently stay freezing, all around controlled, and consistent, but you will be not able to foresee their conduct. Given enough practice when searching for these highlights, you will have the option to spot the boring types of triads under discussion and play it safe against their procedures by utilizing your own (mirroring back).

CHAPTER 32:

Cold Reading

Earlier in the 20th century, during the heyday of scam artists such as fortune tellers and psychic mediums, many people fell victim to cold reading techniques in which the reader would convince people that they knew much more about them than the reader should know. This would lead to a sense of confidence and trust among potential victims, priming them for a performance that would ultimately lead to a hefty fee. Many of these scam artists were enormously successful before investigators and skeptical members of the public were able to debunk them.

Today, these techniques are used in sales settings as a way to gain people's trust by convincing them that the salesperson knows more about what they want than even the customer. Some of the pressure sales tactics that are used in some places are seen as unethical, and many salespeople walk a thin line between being good salespersons and practiced scam artists. At least some of the responsibility falls on people in the general public to be aware and alert when it comes to interacting with salespeople who seem a tad too earnest.

Cold Reading as a term is not new. It was used as early as the 1920s by Edgar Cayce and his associates in terms that referred to the ESP techniques of automatic writing and spirit channeling, all of which have been discredited by modern science. Cayce was performing cold reading by a hundred years or more before he ever coined the term 'cold reading.' In its present sense, cold reading became popular in the 1960s with people such as Joe Dunninger and Sylvia Browne, who both offered psychic readings on television for a fee. Browne is still on television today but out of public sight these days. By the 1970s, cold reading had been given a new name "psychic" or "psychic readings." Today psychic readings are very popular and almost any medium will tell you that they can do it for you, but some videos show no evidence of this at all. There is also a large and growing body of psychology that suggests cold reading techniques can be used to manipulate people.

Cold reader methods include the use of online databases, telephone directories, newspaper articles, or court records to collect information about an individual while pretending to use ESP to uncover the information. The information usually consists of names, dates, places, and events which were known to the client from the client's life or public sources. Cold readers will then relate this information as if it was psychic insight obtained by cold reading techniques.

"Cold reading" can refer to a variety of techniques used by mentalists for tricking their audiences into believing that they have psychic powers. It is also used in a more general sense to describe the tricks used by some fortune tellers (by no means all) to convince people that they are psychic or possess some other unusual ability. While most cold readers will claim only to offer insight into the past and future, they also frequently make claims about the present and even attempt diagnoses of physical ailments or illnesses based on little more than observation.

CHAPTER 33:

Body Language

Body Language

Body language is a significant aspect of modern communications and relationships. From our facial expressions to the movements made by our body, the things that are not said can still convey loads of information.

Experts say that body language may make up about 60% to 65% of all communication.

Learning and understanding body language is essential, but it is necessary that you also consider other clues like context and circumstances. In most cases, you should try looking at the signals as a whole rather than focusing on just a single action.

Understanding how body language works involves learning how to interpret different consistent signals to support or indicate a specific conclusion. Body language is such a powerful concept.

We have learned that Body language is more than just brief descriptions. It encompasses where the body is with the other bodies (this is known as "personal space"). Body language is composed of different body movements, like eye movements and facial expressions.

Additionally, body language also covers everything that we communicate using our body aside from the spoken words, thus encompassing breathing, blood pressure, pulse, blushing, perspiration, etc.

So, body language can be defined as the unconscious and conscious transmission and interpretation of our feelings, our moods, and attitudes through the following:

Posture, movement, position, physical state, and relationship to other bodies or objects.

Facial expressions and even the most precise eye movement.

Origins of Body Language

Over 5 million years ago, approximately 100,000 chimps lived in equatorial Africa. The forests of Africa were starting to dwindle. The climate was hot and dry. These inhabitants were starting to have difficulty finding food, and the trees have become inadequate for them. They had to learn to adapt so they could survive.

The evidence about walking apes was said to have been seen about 4.4 million years ago. Having learned how to walk, these Australopithecines were able to cover a bigger area and find a large variety of food. This ability gave them an evolutionary advantage. But as they reach expanded, life became more complicated.

They began to learn to work in groups to cope with the changes in their environment. They had to learn to interact with others, to know who is an ally and who is an enemy. They had to decide who should be in their group and who is to be excluded.

It was mentally challenging for them. Those who had a smaller brain didn't survive.

During this time, the Homo habilis appeared. They had bigger brains. But having bigger brains meant they needed more energy.

They diversified their food options, and they learned to use stone tools too.

Around 2.5 million years ago, their body still had fur. Part of their socialization was checking out each other's fur. There were about 50 members in each group.

This continued until about 1.7 million years. The size of their brain increased until about 800cc. The increase in their brain size caused also an increase in their body temperature. Eventually, they lost their hair and fur. They developed sweat glands to adapt. In the absence of fur, their skin darkened because of UV radiation. This ushered in the emergence of the Homo Ergaster.

This time saw the beginning of a social shift to male and female bonds. They still lived in groups of 50, and all communication within the group was through the use of body language.

The Homo erectus emerged about 1 million years ago. They started to spread out of Africa. About 500,000 years ago, the second migration by Homo Heidelbergensis to Europe started. This led to the emergence of the Neanderthals some 400,000 years ago. It is interesting to note that the Neanderthals had bigger brains than modern-day humans. They were more muscular and seemed superior to all other "humans."

About 200,000 years ago, our ancestors, the Homo sapiens, emerged.

They were anatomically modern and had a brain size of about 1350+cc.

The Homo sapiens evolved to modern-day humans some 50,000 years ago.

This is a huge time in history, as this is the major turning point with the birth of language.

They faced critical issues during the process of developing a language because of reliability. Primates still used sounds to communicate. Problems arose because it was hard to determine if they could trust a signal or not.

There was always a possibility of the primates faking the signal to benefit themselves. These primates didn't adhere to the concept of morality.

This led to the use of emotionally expressive signals—these are hard to fake.

For humans to be able to communicate without the dangers of deception, they had to create a society around moral regulation. Language and rituals had to co-evolve simultaneously. To know if someone was honest or not, society had to refer to that person's belief and adherence to a particular ritual—this was how religion started.

At this point, humans have begun using body language together with verbal signals as a way to communicate with one another. To self-regulate and prevent deception, they develop religion and rituals. Humans who believed in religion were deemed more trustworthy.

This was how groups were formed. Groups had to learn how to compete against each other to gain access to more resources, gain power, and reproduce and eventually expand. This was also the period when different superstitions came about. Those people who believed in the same superstitions are deemed part of the same group or belief system.

Language enabled humans to increase their groups from 50 to 150. They have learned to verbally conduct social grooming. This also ushered in vocal grooming, which in modern times is called gossip.

Around 50,000 years ago, a small group of humans left Africa and traveled across Asia and Europe. They spread rapidly that about 14,500 years ago, all the other Homo genus became extinct, except for the more superior Homo sapiens.

CHAPTER 34:

Non-verbal Communication

Non-verbal Communication

Non-verbal communication can assume five jobs:

- **Reiteration**: It rehashes and frequently reinforces the message you're making verbally.

- **Logical Inconsistency**: It can negate the message you're attempting to pass on, in this manner, demonstrating to your audience that you may not be coming clean.

- **Replacement**: It can fill in for a verbal message. For instance, your facial demeanor regularly passes on an unmistakably clearer message than words actually can.

- **Supplementing**: It might add to your verbal message. As a chief, if you congratulate a worker, notwithstanding giving acclaim, it can expand the effect of your message.

- **Complimenting**: It might highlight or underline a verbal message.

Beating the table, for instance, can highlight the significance of your message.

Types of Non-verbal Communication

The various kinds of non-verbal communication include:

- Facial expressions
- Body development and stance.

- Signals.
- Eye contact.
- Contact.
- Space.
- Voice.

Characteristics

- Non-verbal communication is omnipresent and multifunctional.
- The CNV can lead to misunderstandings and the opposite too.
- The CNV has phylogenetic and ontogenetic primacy.
- The CNV can express what is not said verbally.
- The CNV is reliable.

In humans, CNV is frequently paralinguistic, that is, it accompanies verbal information by shading it, expanding it, or sending contradictory signals. That is why the CNV is important so far.

When we talk (or listen), our focus is on words rather than body language.

Although our judgment includes both. An audience is simultaneously processing the verbal and non-verbal aspects.

The movements of the body are not generally positive or negative in themselves, rather, the situation and the message will determine its evaluation.

Gestural and Body Language

Head and Face

The first lesson you need to learn in trying to read faces is that they're not honest most of the time. One explanation is that since a young age, we were taught which facial expressions, actions, and behaviors are appropriate for certain occasions and social situations. From that time onwards, we have picked up from experience, which facial expressions draw out the types of reactions we want/expect from other people. Because these facial expressions can be manipulated and made with intention more than any other kind of non-verbal cue.

Arms and Hands

The hands are one of the most important tools you have for communicating; entire languages are made up of simply different hand gestures. Your arms are also important because they can bring people in or build a barrier around you. Your arms are the natural object to use when defending.

Torso

The human torso is universally considered essential to our survival, most importantly because it houses our major organs which need to function efficiently for us to live. Naturally, our instincts are wired to protect this part of the body from harm. It's also important to note that when we're comfortable, we also allow access to our torso. Gestures with the torso that reflect the brain's need to distance oneself and avoid people are good indicators of real feelings.

Legs

If asked which part of the body is the most honest, most people would probably say the eyes or even the face. In reality, Navarro says that it is a person's legs and feet in which the truth lies. Science tells us that millions of years' worth of human evolution have taught us to instinctively keep our legs ready for an escape, especially in situations and environments that endanger our survival. Although for most of our lives, we're trained to smile and pose for the camera control the way we present ourselves in front of the public, and "fake it," this is one thing that remains natural to humans.

The Eyes Speak Volumes

Pay close attention to someone's eyes. If someone is avoiding eye contact, there is a strong possibility that he or she is either uncomfortable, disinterested, nervous, or bored. If the person's pupils appear dilated, it is safe to say that the said person is comfortable and perhaps excited or even likes you.

Read the Face

People will try to conceal and mask their facial expressions to the best of their ability. Sometimes, though, their efforts are not good enough and the body has a way of giving off little telltale signs about what someone is truly thinking. Look for the subtle cues in someone's facial expressions.

Using the Shoulders to Communicate Elegantly

There are many ways to interpret a raised shoulder. It often means that a person is aroused. This is common in highly flirtatious environments such as clubs. A raised shoulder with arms crossed across the body or folded tight means that a person is experiencing extreme fear, anxiety, or tension. He may be cold, too, and just wants to be warmer. This is a defensive position that attempts to minimize the space occupied by a person. By minimizing the space they occupy, they minimize the chances that any threat can notice and harm them. If he raises his shoulders and lowers his head, he wants to protect the neck from any virtual or actual attack. This is the most defensive position, similar to a fetal position before babies are born. People in hiding often assume this position.

Reading the Lips

You are about to discover how to read hidden body language clues through someone's lip movement. Understanding these cues will give you an even deeper insight into what someone is truly trying to convey.

The Analysis of Non-verbal Communication Requires at Least Three Basic Criteria

Every non-verbal behavior is inevitably associated with the whole communication of the person. Even a single gesture is interpreted as a whole, not as something isolated by the members of the interaction. If it is a unique gesture, it is assumed as being a gesture and as a sign that there are no more gestures.

The interpretation of non-verbal movements should be done in terms of their congruence with verbal communication. Normally the emotional intention is revealed by non-verbal movements, and intuitively we can feel the incongruity between them and what we are told verbally. Non-verbal communication needs to be congruent with verbal communication and vice versa so that total communication is understandable and sincere.

The last criterion of interpretation of the meaning of non-verbal communication is the need to place each non-verbal behavior in its communicational context.

CHAPTER 35:

Non-verbal Cues

How to Interpret Non-verbal Communications

Sense People's Presence

People emit energy when they are present in a space, and that energy can be felt by everyone else. An excellent way to recognize this fact is to consider the last time a friend visited your house; you could feel their energy in your home. It is easy to sense someone else's energy in your home because this is a place where you spend a lot of time, so when the energy changes, it is noticeable. Another excellent way to sense people's presence is to think about the different energies between someone, such as the Dalai Lama versus Charles Manson.

Pay Attention to Their Eyes

The age-old saying "Eyes are the window to a person's soul" is true. You can express love, hate, and many other powerful emotions through your eyes. Science has shown that your brain emits electromagnetic signals through the eyes that can be sensed by other people, and vice versa. You can sense this energy anytime you feel someone staring at you, even if you were not originally looking at that person.

Feel Their Physical Touches

A person's physical touches heavily communicate the way they are feeling. The primary points of touch include handshakes, hugging, random touching, and welcomed touching.

Each of these touch-based experiences can communicate significant amounts of energy to you, so pay attention.

Listen to Their Tone and Laugh

You can immediately tell if someone is fake in their communication or laughter, based exclusively on their tones. A person with a tone and laugh that is genuine will come from a deep, centered place, and their voice and laughter will sound hearty and full. If they sound hollow, empty, or forced, they are faking it to cover up what they are feeling or thinking.

You can also hear emotions such as anger, sadness, low confidence, anxiety, insensitivity, and arrogance in a person's voice. Simply through listening to their tone and the way they are enunciating their words, you can pick up on the different emotions in their voice. This particular form of hearing is best achieved by listening to many emotions, which allows you to genuinely hear the differences in emotion. Often, they are so subtle that attempting to explain them would be challenging. A great way to practice hearing emotional energy in a person's voice is to listen to videos or recordings with people that have many different emotions. See if you can identify each emotion as it surfaces and then check to see if your assumption was correct. This way, you can start to pick up on hearing emotional energy in people's voices and laughs.

Sense Their Heart Energy

Each of us has heart energy that we can bring, or leave, from any experience.

When a person brings their heart energy, you feel a sense of fullness around that person. They communicate and behave in ways that make it clear that they have shown up as their full selves and that they feel deeply invested in the present moment. If a person does not bring their heart energy, you can sense that, too, as they seem to be lacking a certain "something." Often, a person that is guarding their heart or purposefully leaving it out of a situation emanates an energy that is ineffable or difficult to describe. Something about them just feels "off" or "missing." If you know a person well, you will be able to quickly tell if their heart is not in it, while people you have just met may require more patience as you learn how to read their unique energy and expressions.

Reading Non-verbal Gestures

Body language is the kind of communication where an individual responds to circumstances through the body, like facial expressions. Among people, more than 54 percent of the time we speak is body expression, 39 percent of the time the speech is used, and just 7 percent of the words spoken. It will be of great benefit to develop one's ability to read and recognize gestures and indications in body language, as this will allow one to understand and interact with other human beings easily.

Body language involves body movements, expressions, eye contact, muscle tension, skin shading, suddenness, and breathing speed. It should be remembered, of course, that the language of the body is different from people and between people of various nationalities and cultures. It is always a good idea to always test what is shown in a person. It may be achieved by answering similar questions and taking attempts to meet others.

Many myths are often asked how to understand the language of the body.

Many deceptive books and internet guides do not say the right thing to men.

There's the fact that you need to learn, while common logic may mislead you into believing that a person's ability to interpret body language is the real secret to deceit. Such essential aspects of body language are:

Pose in most situations, if you do the best posture, you will create the right feeling of men.

The person can make movements with his hands even further.

Defensive people who keep protection often stop facial expressions. One problem is that they have no communication with their ears. It is a role that can also be combined with a person's anxiety or insecurity.

Tell lies. Many telling lies have little or no interaction with the ears. The individual can also keep his or her hands in front of the mouth. The individual may be physical with you, but the mind isn't there. The breathing rate often decreases during this period because the apprehension of telling lies is uncovered. A poker player who bluffed at the pot (speaking a lie) would possibly always reveal these terms.

Non-verbal Cues

Our smiles are one of the most powerful tools we've been given. Non-verbal cues in the form of facial expressions, gestures, and body language can have a tremendous impact on your success or failure in business communications. First impressions have a lot to do with what people think of you and your credibility.

The first impression is what makes someone remember you. The impression is made within five seconds of seeing you for the first time. It's usually based on how you look, how you dress, whether your posture is good, whether you smile or frown… and it's almost always based on non-verbal communication cues.

Understanding Facial Expressions

Facial expressions are an important part of body language. They say a lot about what someone thinks or feels. In every conversation you have, you use your face to communicate with other people, and they use theirs to communicate with you. Being intentional about reading facial expressions is a great opportunity to be aware of what someone else is saying to you and them, so you can say all the right things to land a sale.

When your client does this, be aware of what specific facial expressions they are using. Their eyes, the movement of their mouth, their cheeks, nose, forehead, and even neck all provide insight as to what they are thinking and feeling. Generally speaking, a face that is light and rested indicates someone is relaxed and feeling casual. A face that is scrunched forward indicates anger or disgust, and a face that is stretched outward with raised eyebrows and a dropped jaw indicates surprise or shock.

When you do this, your facial expressions should be used as a way to communicate authority and friendliness. You want to smile, keep soft eyes, and maintain a resting face, but keep a look of confidence in yourself. The easiest way to practice the look of confidence is to go to your bathroom mirror, get in a confident mood, and look at yourself. Then practice making that face regularly. Using this face, alongside a genuine smile and a welcoming look, is an excellent way to create a comfortable environment for your client.

Arms and Torso

Your upper body communicates more than you likely think it does. Being aware of what your upper body is saying is a great way to communicate intentionally, rather than unintentionally. Because your upper body accounts for so much of your overall being, and it is often elaborate in gestures, it is an important part of communication. Be aware of what your arms and torso are saying, and look at your client to see what theirs are saying, too.

When your client does this, pay attention to where their arms are and what direction their torso is facing. If their arms are to the side or actively engaged, and their torso is facing you, this indicates they are with you. Their facial expressions and words can help you determine if they are with you positively or negatively. Naturally, you want them to be with you in a positive way. If your client's arms are crossed, are hanging limp down by their sides, or are behind their back as they clasp their hands behind them, this indicates they are disinterested or not with you. For their torso, if they are leaning toward you, this is a good sign that they are focused and interested in what you have to say. If they are learning away, they are skeptical, disinterested, or getting ready to end the conversation.

When you do this, you want to keep active gestures that are not excessive or overwhelming. Use your hands to communicate or keep them calmly rested in your lap, on your desk, or somewhere else casual. Lean in slightly, and keep your torso pointed toward the person you are talking to, as this creates a sense of interest and connection. When a person feels as though you are addressing them personally, they are far more likely to listen and care about what you have to say.

Legs and Feet

Lastly, you need to pay attention to the legs and feet. Our legs and feet do communicate a lot, though they are not looked at as often as our upper bodies since they are lower and are generally beyond the field of view when we are in an active conversation. Because your legs are less noticeable, you do not have to be quite so focused on them; however, it does help to pay attention so you can add to the overall communication.

When your client does this, the best thing you can do is to pay attention to their feet. Their feet will give you the best information instantly, and without you needing to look down for terribly long. All you need to do is focus on where their feet are pointing, as this tells you what they are most interested in. If their feet are pointed toward you or the product you are selling them, this is a sign that they are engaged with you and are interested in what you have to say. If they are pointed away, especially toward the exit, this means they are looking for a way to end the conversation so they can leave.

When you do this, you should also only worry about keeping your legs neat and your feet pointed in the direction of your interest. In this case, you want to keep at least one foot pointed toward your client, which indicates you are engaged with them. While your client is highly unlikely to consciously recognize this, their subconscious brain will become aware and will use this as a positive cue to indicate a greater sense of security, trust, and connection.

CHAPTER 36:

Using Body Language to Influence

Continuously Make Eye Contact

It is first on the rundown, no ifs, ands, or buts. You will be astounded to take note of that our eyes talk more for our sake. Notwithstanding, this is inclined to some social contrasts. We create trust in what we state and accept the other individual once we visually connect. Our eyes might be the entries to our spirit, however, they are absolutely an approach to build up a relationship and give powerful correspondence. You may state that you are modest and incapable to visually connect more often than not. Indeed, the bashfulness may make you peer down or sideways while imparting. Your crowd may decipher this as an absence of trust in your message. I would encourage you to sustain your eye to eye connection. The beneficial thing about non-verbal communication is that you can learn it with time. Reason to build up the aptitudes bit by bit.

Walk Energetically

Picture the first occasion when you meet anybody. In a languid stance, they come to you, wandering towards you. Picture a similar situation now with an individual strolling with goal and force we're not contemplating running, yet an intentional walk. This simple demonstration is the person's assessment, right? Our strolling style conveys a message of trust and validness and magnificence. At the point when you stroll in certainty, you portray that you understand what you are up to and trust in yourself. You realize what occurs straightaway, individuals will have the option to have faith in you as well.

Draw Out a Reflection

Our emotions and contemplations show up through our non-verbal correspondence, which is the motivation behind this article. At the point when you need to talk better with others, think about mirroring their non-verbal correspondence. This isn't a YouTube preview of a baby imitating someone else, the truth isn't to duplicate or scorn someone, yet rather to show compassion through your non-verbal correspondence. This should be subtle and will take practice, notwithstanding, it can empower your messages to be gotten even more successfully by others.

Allow Individuals to See Their Hands

We all in all use our hands to pass on a message. You can even watch people on the phone, when the other individual can't in any capacity, shape, or see them, using their hands to introduce their significant decision! Right when people can't see our hands, they wonder if we are disguising something if we are restless, and possibly various things. Your hands are a bit of your powerful correspondence; along these lines, use them and keep an essential separation from any negatives that may start from hiding them from others.

Use Empowering Non-Verbal Communication

Two snappy models: eye to eye association is referred to as of now and motioning with people to show that you fathom and also agree. When someone does that it passes on proficiently to you, isn't so correct?

This isn't the fundamental model. Related to reflecting over, this is using our body improvement and movements to show people we think about it and need to check out and acquire from them and that what we are sharing is to their most noteworthy preferred position, as well.

Slow Down

A couple of us accelerate our correspondence. It is prudent to back off, nonetheless, it ruins your signs and advancement. While some speed passes on essentialness, there is a practically unimportant distinction that we cross that drives our non-verbal correspondence to show strain, trepidation, or even abomination. Take a full breath and loosen up a tad.

Have an Incredible Handshake

If you have one, you understand how critical this is. On the off chance that you are unaware of this reality, you may very well have a limp, dead fish, or overpowering and over-controlling handshake. A handshake conveys something explicit about what your character is. Work on a firm and inviting handshake and you will grant authenticity and sureness to others.

While we overall can and should manage these things, see that the recipient of our message, the watcher of our non-verbal correspondence, is the adjudicator. Their perspective on our non-verbal correspondence runs throughout the day. Exactly when we apply the considerations above notwithstanding, we will improve the chances that their insight is sure and will reinforce better correspondences and associations.

Think of learned skills like tying shoes, zipping a coat, and pouring milk into a glass. These were all learned behavior whose nerve pathways are firmly set in the subconscious part of the mind. This part of the brain is the bank of data for all life functions.

CHAPTER 37:

Myths and Misconceptions about Dark Psychology

There are a variety of subjects that are appropriate for dinner discussion. Dark Psychology is not one of them. The last thing you want to know at Thanksgiving is how Uncle Joe performed on his Machiavellian orientation. Due to the maliciousness around Dark Psychology, there are generally very few accessible conversations on the subject.

Take the Dark Triad experiment, for example. Are you thinking of taking it? If so, are you willing to disclose your findings to anyone? The strong odds are that if you responded positively to the first query, you would presumably respond negatively to the second question. Many people want to speak of themselves as decent citizens.

Furthermore, they want other people to think of them as nice individuals. Putting your Dark Triad evaluation on a show for everyone to see might not help this objective. Because of all this hush-hush around Dark Psychology, there are, however, several assumptions and misconceptions concerning character traits that are critical to Dark Psychology.

Myth One

Psychopaths and sociopaths are the same things.

Truth

Psychopathy and sociopathy are two distinct forms of antisocial personality conditions.

The words "psychopath" and "sociopath" are used synonymously in daily conversation. However, the two characteristics are very distinct from each other and there are some differences between these two personality disorders. Experts find sociopathy to be a less severe condition than psychopathy. The list below illustrates some of the features that differentiate a psychopath from a sociopath.

Psychopath

I. Lacks moral scruples.

II. They are willing to fit in by being attractive and are therefore more difficult to spot.

III. Cold-hearted and highly tactical.

Sociopath

I. Has a poor conscience.

II. Don't have any intention of fitting in and are therefore easy to identify. Will only be concerned about them in the first place.

III. Hot-headed, trying to jump without checking.

Myth Two

Psychopaths are born and are not raised.

Truth

Psychopaths are indeed born that way.

Psychopathy is a very complex personality disorder that more often than not begins at birth. Psychopaths emerge out of the womb, already programmed to behave differently from most people. As a consequence, they move away from what is normal and often find themselves in situations in which any other "average" individual would not typically find them. A study has shown that the psychopath's brain functions in a different manner relative to the brains of other individuals who do not have any personality disorders. So, what happens when a psychopath is born?

Depending on the type of setting in which the psychopath emerges, they will grow into one of the following pathways. If a toddler who exhibits indications of psychopathy grows up in a supportive family, he or she would be expected to become a corporate or political figure with a lot of power. If the infant grows up in a dysfunctional or abusive setting, he or she is likely to become a serial killer or murderer. Psychopaths who are molded in an atmosphere that is somewhere between the first two conditions end up in positions of control in areas such as law enforcement and administration.

Myth Three

Sociopaths are born that way.

Truth

Sociopaths are primarily the result of their surroundings.

More often than not, sociopaths are the product of the society in which they are raised. It often begins with a biological or hereditary propensity to sociopathy, which is then compounded by the form of care they receive. For example, a boy who grows up in a society where nobody appears to care for him is likely to have the same lack of sympathy for others in his later life. When children grow up around parents who possess little sense of morality and have no social code, their morals will be profoundly weakened as a result.

Myth Four

Women cannot be psychopaths.

Truth

There are reported cases of female psychopaths.

More often than not, when you hear the word "psychopath" you immediately assume it is a male character. Instead, they utilize their sexuality and womanhood to exploit others. Female psychopaths also tend to have a large number of intimate partners.

Myth Five

Psychopaths are fascinated with murder.

Truth

Psychopaths are enthusiasts.

Murder is just one of the ways that psychopaths quench their need for exhilaration. When most people think about psychopaths, they think of the massacres that happen left, right, and center.

Though while a murderer may be more likely than not to be a psychopath, it is also clear that some psychopaths are no more likely than the majority of the citizenry to commit murder. Most psychopaths go through their life in pursuit of thrills, but never really cause violent damage to anyone.

Yes, they could break a few hearts when they hop from one romantic partner to another and throw a few people under the bus to scale the professional ladder, but that is as far as many of them go. If you are searching for a psychopath in your life, you are unlikely to find one if you are only searching for brutality and lust for blood.

Myth Six

Psychopathy is a mental disorder that can be treated.

Truth

Psychopathy is a personality disorder that has no treatment.

If it were a mental disorder, there would be a chance of therapy. Psychopathy, however, is a personality disorder, and this means that no treatment would make psychopaths calm, emotional, and empathetic. Because they don't accept that something is wrong with them either, they would not even be concerned about medication, even if it did exist.

In situations where psychopaths have been persuaded to try therapy to fix broken relationships, it is not unusual to find them trying to manipulate the other party into believing that the therapy is effective or has already worked.

Note that these people are extremely deceptive and capable of using whatever methods are necessary to overcome challenging circumstances. Owing to their brazen lack of fear and compassion, a psychopath will have no trouble wasting a loved one's time in therapy, if only to make it seem like they are trying.

Myth Seven

You can transform an individual on the Dark Triad by treating them appropriately.

Truth

Most of the individuals who rank highly on the Dark Triad evaluation continue so for the remainder of their lives. Love is a curious phenomenon in that it lets people feel that they are capable of the impossible, even though the truth is revealed before their eyes. Manipulative characters have a way of love-bombing you into assuming that they are the perfect match that you have been looking for all along. Sadly, this is typically just an effort to draw you into a friendship that is simply smoke and mirrors. When someone has gotten into this kind of partnership, and the true character of the manipulator then surfaces, in many cases, you will see a romantic partner hanging around with the belief that things will improve and love will be sufficient to turn things around. Unfortunately, this is mostly never the case.

First of all, the fact that psychopathy is mostly inherited indicates that it is impossible to overcome it. At best, psychopaths can only turn their lack of empathy into goals that are not harmful to social structure as a whole. As for Machiavellianism and narcissism, these often derive from profound psychological distress that may take a great deal of strategy to conquer. Most people are going to lean heavily towards Machiavellianism and narcissism as a defensive mechanism. Every effort to get them out of this state will only appear to them as an assault, leading them to mount their resistance. As such, interference in the form of love can be extremely inefficient. It is also important to remember that love and other shimmering feelings are not necessarily highly rated by a person in the Dark Triad. They may not even recognize love, regardless of how it seems. As such, if you are in a relationship with a partner who has the traits of the Dark Triad, you might want to reconsider whether that is what you desire.

Myth Eight

Individuals who rank high on the Dark Triad are more alluring.

Truth

This has been proven to be false.

Why is it that people still tend to be drawn towards the narcissists and the psychopaths of this world? Is it because the Dark Triad characters are more appealing than most of us? In an attempt to ascertain if Dark Triad characters are better-looking, academic scholars have investigated a variety of individuals with higher Dark Triad ratings. The findings of this research indicated that the main reason why these participants looked appealing was that they dressed and portrayed themselves physically in a way that was well organized. When they were clothed in bland clothing, these individuals didn't seem as appealing as before. As such, it is almost reasonable to believe that the care and energy that goes into getting dressed and the confidence that comes with it are what renders a narcissist or psychopath more appealing than they are.

Myth Nine

Psychopaths can improve when they have children.

Truth

Psychopaths are unable to be empathic or responsible for their offspring.

Psychopaths typically have a very difficult time raising their children. Unlike average parents who are not on the Dark Triad scale, it is challenging for psychopaths to view their children as different individuals. Rather, they perceive them to be devices or extensions of themselves that are accessible for their use whenever they wish. Psychopaths are more inclined to see their children as achievements that make them feel good than as young, emotionally fragile beings who are looking for somebody to protect them throughout their early lives. As such, a psychopath will usually force their children to develop skills in something they have no desire to participate in, even though it may be to the detriment of the children's mental health and development. They could forcefully sign them up for swimming classes, for example, as they feel that their child will become an excellent swimmer and a champion, just to boost their social status in the neighborhood. It is very difficult to convince psychopathic parents to see that they are used to excelling only themselves and they will not comprehend why their children will not do whatever it takes to get to the highest level.

Myth Ten

You are either on the Dark Triad, or you are not.

Truth

The Dark Triad is a scale on which some feature highly, while others appear further down.

The characteristics of narcissism, psychopathy, and Machiavellianism are rooted in every individual. The only distinction is that in some individuals, these behaviors are amplified to the extent that they often become toxic to those around them. Take narcissism, for example. Everyone has their own way of thinking about themselves. You are more likely than not to choose to have decent thoughts about yourself. You like to think that you are nice-looking, intelligent, and easy to love. For a narcissist, this self-image is taken out of context to the point that their entire life circles around it.

CHAPTER 38:

Mind Control and Emotional Influence

Various Techniques of Mind Control in Society

In this day and age, there are ten versions of mind control that exist. These are essentially modern-day versions of the techniques you learned about in the "history of mind control." They understand these strategies and how they will assist you in understanding how they contribute to mind control. After, you will learn about the techniques you can employ and how they work as well!

Education

By educating impressionable children, society essentially teaches them to become "ideal" members of the community.

They are taught and trained in specific ways that fulfill the government and authorities' desires, and most people don't even think twice about it.

Advertising and Propaganda

By putting advertising and propaganda everywhere, those in control can eliminate people's feeling of self-worth and encourage them to need what is being sold, as opposed to just wanting it.

This is essentially a subliminal strategy to make people feel poorly about themselves, to purchase whatever is being advertised, to increase their feelings of self-worth.

Predictive Programming

The idea of predictive programming is essential for authorities to place references to significant activities in the popular media before the atrocity ever occurs.

As a result, everyone already warmed up to the idea, and so they are not overly fearful when it takes place. It is essentially a foreshadowing tactic used on real humans instead of in writing.

Sports, Politics, Religion

The idea of these strategies is to "divide and conquer." Ultimately, each one has people placed into various categories, where they feel very strongly.

As a result, they don't support one another, but instead, they are against each other. This means that they are divided, and so the authority can conquer.

Food, Water, Air

Believe it or not, many toxins and additives are put into food, water, and air that are changing the makeup of your brain.

As a result, you are being subjected to mind control every time you consume anything essential to your livelihood.

Drugs

Whether they are street drugs or pharmaceutical drugs, they can alter your brain's chemicals and therefore change your mind.

Drugs can be considered akin to old-time lobotomies, shock chairs, and other mind control types to eliminate mental illness from people. Only these days, they are much more commonly accepted and are taken by people everywhere.

Military Testing

The military has tested mind control for a long time, claiming that they want to use it as an opportunity to control the opponent and ward off any violence.

They have even discussed creating helmets that would protect the militia from mind control strategies and focus on their missions.

Electromagnetic Spectrum

This essentially means the electromagnetic rays that are cast by electronic devices.

We all have our houses filled with them, and every time you plug them in or use them, you are subjected to the electromagnetic spectrum. It is believed that this can have a mind-altering effect that would contribute to mind control.

Television, Computer, "Flicker Rate"

Televisions and computers are believed to subject people to overwhelming amounts of information and ideas that ultimately cause them to be hypnotized by the ideas and lull the information into their subconscious minds, thus creating mind control.

There are also "flicker rates," which means essentially that data is flickering by faster than the eye can see. It is believed that these strategies, including video games, are used to execute mind control strategies.

Nanobots

These are ultimately placed into your brain and used to alter your mind. They believe that by putting a nanobot into your brain, they can create any outcome they desire because you are under mind control. You can literally "press a button and become happy."

Understanding the various forms of mind control can help show you the many ways it can be done. While some of these may be chalked up to conspiracy theories, you can still derive a general understanding of how each strategy would contribute to mind control. When you learn to master mind control, you must understand all the different ways it can occur.

In the above scenarios, there were some common trends. The general ones included: subliminal messages, mental overwhelm, education, and direct physical altering of the mind. These are the most common methods used to attempt to brainwash someone and control their mind.

Some of these strategies are not doable for the average person; however, understanding them will help you prevent yourself from being subject to mind control.

In the meantime, we will focus on three primary methods of mind control that you can use and quickly execute on virtually anyone. They include persuasion, manipulation, and deception.

These methods are all strategies that are completed using the spoken word, and they can assist you in altering someone's mind so that you can have your desired effect on them. Now, you will learn about each one.

Mind Control Techniques

Present-day mind control is both innovative and mental. Tests demonstrate that, by uncovering the techniques for mind control, the impacts can be diminished or disposed of, at any rate for mind control publicizing and promulgation. Increasingly hard to counter are the physical interruptions, which the military-mechanical complex keeps on creating and enhance.

1. Education has consistently been an eventual tyrant's absolute dream to "teach" usually receptive youngsters. Subsequently, it has been a focal segment to Communist and Fascist oppressive regimes from the beginning of time. Nobody has been increasingly instrumental in uncovering the motivation of present-day instruction than Charlotte Iserbyt—one can start an investigation into this region by downloading her book as a free PDF, The Deliberate Dumbing Down of America, revealing the job of Globalist establishments in forming a future planned to deliver servile automatons reigned over by a wholly taught, mindful exclusive class.

2. **Promotions and Propaganda** – Edward Bernays has been referred to as the creator of the consumerist culture that was planned principally to focus on individuals' mental self-portrait (or scarcity in that department) to transform a need into a need. This was at first imagined for items, for example, cigarettes, for instance. Nonetheless, Bernays also noted in his 1928 book, Propaganda, that "purposeful publicity is the imperceptible government's official arm." This can be seen most unmistakably in the advanced police state and the developing native nark culture, enveloped with the pseudo-enthusiastic War on Terror. The expanding union of media has empowered the whole corporate structure to converge with the government, which currently uses the idea of promulgation arrangement. Media; print, motion pictures, TV, and link news would now be able to work flawlessly to incorporate a general message that appears to have the ring of truth since it originates from such a significant number of sources simultaneously. When one moves toward becoming sensitive to recognizing the fundamental "message," one will see this engraving all over. What's more, this isn't even to specify subliminal informing.

3. **Prescient Programming** – Many still deny that prescient writing computer programs is genuine. Innovative programming has its causes in predominately elitist Hollywood, where the big screen can offer a significant vision of where society is going. For a nitty-gritty breakdown

of explicit models, Vigilant Citizen is an incredible asset that will most likely make you take a gander at "amusement" in a unique light.

4. **Sports, Politics, Religion** – Some may resent seeing religion, or even legislative issues, put together with sports as a technique for mind control.

The focal topic is the equivalent all through: isolate and prevail. The systems are very straightforward: they impede individuals' common propensity to participate for their endurance and train them to frame groups bowed on control and winning. Sports have consistently had a job as a critical diversion that corrals innate propensities into a non-significant occasion. In present-day America has arrived at silly extents where challenges will break out over a game VIP leaving their city. Yet, fundamental human issues, for example, freedom, are chuckled away, is immaterial.

5. **Food, Water, and Air** – Additives, poisons, and other nourishment harms modify mind science to make mildness and indifference. Fluoride in drinking water has been demonstrated to bring down IQ; Aspartame and MSG are excitotoxins that energize synapses until they kick the bucket, and simple access to the inexpensive food that contains these toxins, by and large, has made a populace that needs center and inspiration for a functioning way of life. The vast majority of the cutting-edge world is flawlessly prepped for uninvolved responsiveness—and acknowledgment—of the authoritarian tip top.

6. **Medications** — we can equate this to any addictive substance; however, mind controllers' mission is to be sure you are dependent on something. One noteworthy arm of the cutting-edge mind control motivation is psychiatry, which expects to characterize all individuals by their issue instead of their human potential. Today, it has been taken to considerably assist limits as medicinal oppression has grabbed hold where everybody has a type of confusion—especially the individuals who question authority. The utilization of nerve tranquilizers in the military

has prompted record quantities of suicides. To top it all off, the cutting—edge medication state currently has over 25% of U.S. youngsters on mind-desensitizing drugs.

7. **Military testing** — there is a long history associated with the military as the proving ground for mind control.

8. **Electromagnetic range** — an electromagnetic soup encompasses all of us, charged by present-day gadgets of comfort which have been appeared to affect mind work directly. In an implicit affirmation of what is conceivable, one scientist has been working with a "divine being head protector" to instigate dreams by adjusting the mind's electromagnetic field. Our advanced soup has us latently washed by conceivably mind-changing waves.

Simultaneously, a broad scope of potential outcomes, for example, phone towers, is currently accessible to the eventual personality controller for more straightforward mediation.

Mind control is more common than most people think. It is not easy to detect because of its subtle nature. In many instances, it happens under what is perceived as normal circumstances like through education, religion, TV.

Programs, advertisements, and so much more. Cults and their leadership use mind control to influence their members and control whatever they do. It is not easy to detect mind control. However, when one realizes it, they can get out and start again.

CHAPTER 39:

The Process of Mind Control

Ten Modern and Common Mind Control Strategies

Manipulation can produce various outcomes and is used for multiple reasons, from compliance and obedience to influencing how a person looks at themselves or others to evoke individual responses and behaviors. Essentially, when your actions and behaviors are influenced heavily by an individual or group, you may often dismiss your doubts or feelings in favor of theirs. The effects of mind control don't work immediately in most cases, as this would be too obvious and easy to spot.

How does mind control work? Mind control is the desired result of manipulation and related psychological techniques or methods that effectively influence your emotions and mind to bend your will and actions for another person's gain. It can be used to gain power, influence, money, or benefits from another person, and maybe applied towards people in a position of privilege or a state of vulnerability, making them a prime target.

Once a person establishes a level of trust and confidence over another, they can be "primed" or targeted for mind control. The person seeking this form of dominance may be observant in the other person's habits and behaviors, learning how best to bait them with favorable comments and responses to gain their trust for further manipulation. Mind control and manipulation are almost always used for exploitation purposes. They often begin with seemingly more benign versions of persuasion or coaxing, which later develop into more potent forms of manipulative techniques.

1. Gaslighting

This is the technique used to see if the person's words sound like his actions. Gaslighting is a method that can be used to question the personality's belief. With time, the person has to understand the use of this tool to use the manipulation effectively. There is a set of questions among the public, used by the manipulator to dodge the questions' essence. The entire scenario of the public changes with time because of the gas questions asked by the manipulator.

2. Generalizations

The generalizations of a manipulator are a strong sense of demotivation for the public to withstand. The manipulator easily generalizes all the terms and tactics employed on a social, economic, and political factor, and the generalizations come with time. The stereotypes are important enough for a manipulator to understand the essence of all compatible reasons for the public. With time, the manipulator can see the distance of the people go far away. Therefore, the public's reach from the real cause defines the manipulator's status, and the manipulator can control a lot of sense through it. Therefore, the use of a generalizing matter creates more and more aspects for the students and civilians. Thus, generalization gives impetus to the manipulator, and with time, it can be more asserted in the coming. So, conception can lead to a lot of trouble and menace for the student.

3. Moving the Goal Post

The manipulators have every right to deny your goal and ambition. They call it the moving of goal post, and this is how the public can induce a flawed and obscene mechanism to it. The goal post is the ambition of every man to cater to the fundamentally obsessed question of the incident, and with time, the manipulator tends to de-track you from the quest at the earliest. Therefore, the track is a sense of motivation for you, and you do not get enough aspiration for the students and civilians. The idea is quite simply that the public can create more satisfaction for the people, and with time, the manipulators induce havoc.

4. Changing the Subject

The manipulator would do his best in changing the subject. This aspect makes them avoid accountability for their previous actions, and with time, he learns the act of betrayal and deception. Any time or place where he cannot see the masterpiece of the subject, he tends to foil with the public. Therefore, he is not even governing the public's matter so that he could not even to the point of appreciation. Thus, changing the subject of any conversation is also a tool of manipulation required by all means necessary.

5. Name-Calling

Name-calling is an art and tactic that can be used to induce marginalization in the incident, and with time, it could lead to dilemmas and destruction. The name-calling starts with a mode of aspiration for the pupils but ends in utter devastation for the public. This concept can be easily seen in many areas, and portions of the world, and such a practice can induce horror and terror in the region.

This practice of name-calling can be used in the factors that enable one with destruction and devastation.

6. Smear Campaigns

This campaign is used to address the horrendous use of psychology for the public. This is a play in which you are the victim, and they are the martyr. According to them, you have displayed a sense of lousy relationship with them, and for that mere reason, they have labeled you as a dead person. You no longer have a sense of reputation in the system, and every time you encounter them, they tend to call you wrong and the gone one. This aspect has many difficulties for you, and you end up being a psychopath. This aspect has emotional issues for you, psychological problems for you, ovulational, and many more. Therefore, smear campaigns are personally made to make you feel wrong and obscene, and with time, you feel very hectic.

7. Devaluation

This devaluation is not the currency devaluation, but it is the human devaluation of yourself; you tend to be very bad and obsolete in your character that you embarrass everyone's exes. You will as it is your applicable duty to make the lives and ages of others feel embarrassing, and with time, you control over your anger to inflict punishment among the others. For instance, there was a time when people could cooperate and could not try to defame others. However, with the burgeoning social media, people tend to decide others' relationships by making them feel very degenerate. This is the crucial aspect of psychology, which could be very tumultuous for you, and with time, he felt terrible and worse. Therefore, devaluation is meant to be an outlet of Mind Control, and it can be very harmful to anyone who does it.

8. Aggressive Jokes

Aggressive Jokes are the modes to make others look small and in chaos. These jokes could be anything like the jokes on individuality, the jokes on society, and the jokes on caste. These jokes impose derogatory remarks on the individuals, and with time, the individuals feel very bad about them. The idea is simply that psychology believes that manipulators could be the worst nightmares for innocent personalities. People can use the tower of others to personally sabotage the concept of friendliness and equality among the persons. With time, people tend to showcase a system of defamation, among others. Thus, aggressive jokes can be harmful and hazardous to others.

9. Triangulation

This is the concept in which the individuals tend to use others' supposed threat to manipulate the innocents. Suppose there are three individuals in a room, two of them are arguing about anything, and the person sitting next to them is of a high caste. The manipulator would use the tower of the supposed threat of the third person to deter that of a second person, and with time, the concept of triangulation would be bolstered. Hence, the use of force and manipulation makes the third parties very bad and degenerate.

10. Use of Tools

These are sensory devices, visual sensors, automatic assembly, industrial manipulators, and photoelectric detectors. These tools cast a shadow of degeneration among the personalities, and with time, the people can have a list of traumata embedded in them. Therefore, with time, the tools can be used for a stringent version of the collaboration.

Thus, these are some of the ways and tools of manipulation that can harbor evil deeds in the person.

CHAPTER 40:

Common Techniques of Mind Control

Standard Techniques of Mind Control

Mind control is a term that is used for several psychological phenomena such as mind control, coercive control, brainwashing, coercive persuasion, malignant use of group dynamics, and a lot more.

It is a psychological theory with many names. The many names given to the theory are a clear indication of the fact that there is a lack of agreement which makes room for distortion and confusion, especially in the hands of those that intend to make use of it covertly for their selfish interests.

There are different ways which people use to control the minds of others; below are some of these techniques:

Subliminal Messaging

These are either visual or auditory messages sent to a receiver's brains to bypass the person's everyday conscious perceptions. To do this effectively, the mind controller flashes these messages to the other person's brain without giving the person's eyes the chance to capture/see the image or make sounds inaudible to the receiver's ears.

The messages are sent directly to the brain. The mind controller aims to influence the other person, and they do that effectively using this technique.

Brainwave Synchronization

For everything a person does or thinks, there is a league of neurons that communicate with each other in the brain. These neurons generate and transmit electrical signals between themselves, creating patterns in the form of waves, known as brainwaves. For different states of mind of a person, there are different resultant frequencies of these brainwaves.

Thus, the question becomes whether it is possible to get to a predetermined state of mind.

Neuro-Linguistic Programming (Nlp)

This is a technique that has its basis in the idea that successful behavioral patterns can be made possible in either the self or other people by modifying underlying thought patterns and interpersonal relationships or interactions.

Cognitive Behavioral Therapy

This is a therapeutic technique that may not be related to mind control. Still, it works perfectly when it comes to the underlying principle of modifying a person's behavior, known as behavioral modification, based on corresponding thought modification.

Hypnosis

This is a mind-control tool that professional hypnotists use to fish out a person's suggestible subconscious mind by moving past the conscious and analytical mind to create positive thoughts or replace old negative beliefs that the reason has held onto for a long time.

People in sports have used hypnosis successfully. It has also been used in other fields like education, therapy, and self-improvement to boost a person's self-confidence and get rid of phobias, fears, and bad habits.

It is used for relaxation and stress relief too.

According to the National Institute of Health, hypnosis is a useful tool in reducing some kinds of pain, which include the pain from cancer.

Also, hypnosis has been proven to have some self-help benefits. It has been said to be a useful tool in any attempt to change another person's thought process for things like persuasion, negotiation, or sales.

When hypnosis is used in this manner, it is known as conversational hypnosis, based on the techniques created/developed by the American psychiatrist and medical hypnotherapist Milton H. Erickson.

CHAPTER 41:

The Art of Reading People

Human beings are regarded to be among the most complex creatures on earth.

The complexity of human beings extends to the nature of their behavior.

This implies that it is quite difficult to fully understand and Read such behavior, especially from a layman's perspective.

Psychiatrists have the upper hand when it comes to their capacity to understand and Read human behavior.

This is because they have the pre-requisite training that equips them with the capacity to Read such behavior in a much more professional manner.

However, you do not have to be a psychiatrist to understand human behavior.

Anyone with adequate information on some of the fundamental issues that underlie human behavior can effectively and accurately Read such behavior.

Enhanced capacity to Read human behavior will enable you to have a greater understanding of the people around you.

Sometimes, people might not be willing to go out and actually say what is on their minds.

However, when you know what to look for concerning both verbal and non-verbal cues, you will be able to decipher the message that they are trying to put across, thus eliminating potential conflicts that can arise due to miscommunication.

It is also equally important to maintain an open mind and avoid any pre-established biases that can undermine your capacity to fully grasp and Read what the other person is trying to put across.

Use of Language

One of the most distinguishing aspects when it comes to how people behave is their preferred use of language.

Language is considered the most reliable universal tool for communication.

Language also plays a key role in fostering relations among people since it enables them to communicate freely, exchange ideas, and express their perspectives on different issues.

However, how different people use language is different, and these differences usually reflect their behavior and attitudes towards various things.

The preference for polite language is one thing that can enable you to Read the behavior of the person you are communicating with.

Heavy use of polite words and expressions such as please, may I, kindly and other such words that are meant to convey a message of politeness can go a long way in helping one Read human behavior.

People who prefer to use such words and expressions tend to put a lot of value and emphasis on positive human relations and would be more than willing to take into account the perspectives of others.

Such individuals are usually polite and considerate towards others and are more likely to make a compromise to accommodate the needs of the other person.

On the other hand, the absence of polite words and expressions could be an indicator that the person is likely to exhibit dictatorial tendencies towards others.

This implies that such an individual is more likely to insist on having their way at any cost and not consider the option of making any compromises.

When it comes to using language, another aspect that comes out strongly is also the preference for unconventional, harsh, or abusive language.

For instance, curse words are mainly considered to be an unconventional language and are not used in mainstream communication.

However, there are people whose usage of such words is much more common as compared to others.

Preference for curse words, abusive language, and harsh words can be helpful in the analysis of human behavior since people who prefer such language are usually more prone to violent behavior towards others.

Similarly, the preference for such words can also indicate that someone is likely to pay little attention to the consequences of their actions.

A good example would be an employee who uses such words against the employer.

In such a scenario, such an employee might end up adopting an overall lackluster attitude towards their roles and responsibilities because they do not care whether or not they will get fired.

Finally, such people can also adopt an overall resigned attitude towards life, and this can undermine the relationships that they have with their family members, friends, and other people who are significant in their lives.

Interpretation of Non-Verbal Cues

People might not often say what is really on their minds.

In some cases, someone might say one thing while in essence, they mean the opposite.

For instance, one might say that they are satisfied with a reward that they have been offered, but in reality, they are highly unsatisfied with the same.

In such a situation, your capacity to identify non-verbal cues can go a long way in facilitating accurate analysis of the behavior of the person that you are communicating with.

This is because such non-verbal cues offer a window into the exact position and opinion that a person has towards something.

Facial Expression

There are several non-verbal cues that you can use to Read human behavior with one of them being reading of another person's facial expression.

It is very easy for someone to lie with their mouths, but quite difficult to do the same with their face.

Facial expression can depict the actual feeling that has on a certain issue.

Facial expression can depict happiness, sadness, anger, disgust, and even resentment.

When you know exactly what to look for in terms of facial expressions, you will be in a better position to know what a person feels and how they will behave when they are subjected to a certain situation.

For instance, a spouse might indicate that they are happy with you going away on your holiday for a while.

However, their facial expression might indicate that they are unhappy with your decision.

Your capacity to decipher such an expression will enable you to know how they are likely to behave while you are away, such as engaging in an activity that you might not approve of.

Raised Eyebrows

Some of the most notable facial expressions that most people overlook include raising of the eyebrows, which mainly shows that someone is surprised by a suggestion or an opinion.

At times, a raised eyebrow might indicate that someone is in doubt regarding the viability of the suggestion.

For instance, you might put forward a suggestion for a weekend activity, and they accept but a raised eyebrow.

This implies that they are in doubt and are therefore not likely to embrace the suggestion, even though they have indicated their approval.

Such a friend will, therefore, exhibit behavior that contradicts their earlier position, such as failing to pick up your calls even after repeated attempts.

Frown Lines

In addition to raised eyebrows, another facial expression that you can look out for is the presence and nature of frown lines.

A high concentration of frown lines might be an indicator that the person is deeply concerned about something.

Such an individual might not be willing to share their concerns with you, but in case you notice such frown lines then you will be in a position to know that they might be faced with some serious issue in their lives.

Clenched Teeth

Clinched teeth also fall within the category of facial expression that can be used as a non-verbal cue.

Many people will clench their teeth if they are uneasy with a situation that they are in.

Whenever you are interacting with someone with clenched teeth, then you can look for ways of making them feel at ease, thus making the interaction more productive.

Body Language

Body Posture

In addition to facial expression, another non-verbal cue that can be quite helpful in Reading the behavior of others is body language.

Your body language says a lot about what you are thinking and how you are likely to behave.

Body language refers to several things such as your posture, the use of gestures, and even your proximity to the person you are communicating with.

A posture can tell a lot about the character of a person and consequently, their general behavior.

For instance, people who prefer to communicate while putting their arms across their chest are more likely to keep things close to themselves.

Such people are least likely to lie about issues that affect them in their personal lives or even volunteer information that might have a significant impact on the people that they are communicating with.

On the contrary, more open-minded people will prefer more informal postures, such as putting their hands behind their heads in a relaxed fashion while communicating with others.

Such individuals are more likely to embrace new ideas, focus on the issues that the other person is highlighting, and even offer alternative perspectives to encourage a more productive discussion.

Body language can, therefore, be used in Reading how someone else is likely to respond to other people and their ideas.

Proximity

Proximity is also another aspect of body language that is very important when it comes to body language.

Proximity in this context refers to how close two people are when they are physically interacting with one another.

People who are not willing to fully engage with the other person would prefer to lean away while talking to them.

A good example would be a colleague leaning away from you when you are discussing a business proposal with them.

In this scenario, the colleague might show approval of your proposal, but the fact they were leaning away from you might result in contradictory behavior on their part.

They are thus more likely to end up rejecting the idea after all.

On the other hand, someone who is interested in the idea is likely to lean forward during your conversation, ask follow-up questions, and nod their heads in approval.

Such body language indicates genuine acceptance, and thus, the individual will go out of their way and work hand in hand with you in ensuring that the proposal is indeed a success.

The Positioning of the Arms

The position of the arms is an important aspect of body language that you should always look out for.

In many cases, people will expose their arms while communicating.

The arms can also be used to illustrate gestures and other elements of non-verbal communication.

However, there are situations in which the other party might opt to place their arms in a position that is away from you, for instance, hiding their arms under the table.

In such a scenario, the person is more likely to be hiding something from you.

Similarly, hiding the arms can also indicate that the person does not hold their same opinion as you do on the issue at hand, but their approval is mainly meant to impress or manipulate you.

CHAPTER 42:

Human Behavior

How to Read Human Behavior?

Probably the greatest puzzle of humanity is finding the key to how to peruse individuals' brains. When you could examine individuals' contemplations, you could know precisely what someone else is thinking. The intensity of mind perusing traps and methods truly lies in your capacity by the way you are reading the conduct and flag that the other individual gives you. Here are the mystery approaches to understand individuals' musings through non-verbal communication. When you recognize what an individual is supposing, you are in control of fantastic information that can enable you to lead cooperation to support you.

Perusing non-verbal communication is fun and straightforward. A large portion of us doesn't do this deliberately, so we neglect to perceive precisely what an incredible personality perusing procedure it is. Here are a few things to watch out for to kick you off:

If they are confronting you, they are tuning in and focusing on you. In any case, if they are dismissed, they are not centered on you. When they are shaking side to side, they are anxious and need to end the conversation. A turned back is an indication of purposely overlooking or staying away from somebody.

When somebody backs up, on an intuitive level, they feel undermined and are withdrawing from you. If somebody is step by step moving towards you, they are keen on you or what you are stating.

Pointing their knees or their feet towards you is a widespread consent to they are in arrangement with you, they are adjusting their stance to yours.

If they start to imitate your non-verbal communication, that is an indication that you are driving the discussion.

Crossed arms are an indication of preventiveness or disdain, the particular case is the point at which the thumbs are unmistakably visible and pointing upwards, which implies they are feeling disconnected yet friendly.

If their hands are confronting you with open palms, at that point they are accessible/responsive to what you are stating.

If eyes look upward to one side, they are attempting to take a picture of nothing. They are effectively utilizing their creative mind, and this can be an indication that they are making up whatever they are disclosing to you. If their eyes look upwards to one side, they are attempting to recall a specific picture, get to a particular memory. These are only the typical rules, a few people, particularly the left-gave, have the contrary eye developments, so it's essential to get a standard perusing by convincing them to recollect something that you know occurred. A large portion of these things we will feel during our collaborations. Without giving mindful consideration, we will begin to sense when an individual is getting to be cautious and at precisely that point see their shut non-verbal communication. Figuring out how to focus on your sentiments is a simple method to begin ending up progressively mindful of what the non-verbal communication of others is letting you know.

Besides sociopaths and constant liars, double-dealing is distressing. When we are worried, blood flow is organized to the essential organs and occupied away from the limits. If somebody is lying, they are in all respects prone to have cold hands. This pressure will likewise make the individual progressively anxious because of a loud clamor or some other alarm. In any case, recollect, stress does not suggest trickery.

Eye contact when we are lying isn't frequent. However, it very well may be constrained. When an individual begins looking that feels off, at that point, they are presumably angling toward something obscure. How an individual is thinking will be reflected in the words they use and the inquiries they pose. Somebody who likes to discuss social circumstances and connections is somebody who is centered around relational connections and will react much better to associations that consolidate those components. Relationships depend on feelings, and these individuals will be influenced more by enthusiastic contentions than legitimate ones.

By focusing on every one of the signs an individual is accidentally radiating, you will appear to peruse their brain. These methods will give you a familiarity with what others are feeling that you may even begin to astonish yourself with your precision. The vast majority are so centered around what they are going to state straightaway or what they look for from communication that they are just redirecting an exceptionally modest quantity of their thoughtfulness regarding the other individual. When we center our complete consideration around what the other individual is doing and saying, we increase enormous understanding into what they are thinking, however, how they believe.

Instructions to Read People like A Book

Find how to peruse individuals like a book, and you will most likely accomplish quite a lot more with other individuals. When you comprehend what is happening within them, at that point, you can impact, induce, and even personality control them.

How you do that is by figuring out how to perceive particular character examples and manners by which they structure their inside experience.

For instance, you can distinguish whether somebody is an individual who can deal with weight well and can keep his cool even in pressure circumstances. There are three principal ways for how individuals react to pressure: enthusiastic, picking, or thinking. Passionate individuals are the individuals who get tossed into specific sentiments, and after that can do nothing about it. Picking individuals are the individuals who at first experience the sentiments, yet then they choose to remove themselves from them and work things through sensibly. And afterward, there are the individuals who don't react genuinely by any stretch of the imagination - they act judiciously, legitimately, and thoroughly consider things immediately.

One way you can do this is to get some information about a work circumstance where they experienced inconvenience. Enthusiastic individuals will remember the experience somewhat - you can hear the feelings in their manner of speaking, you can perceive how the muscles in their face worry, their body stance, or signals may change. For decision individuals, you may at first observe that; however, and then they go again into the unbiased state. Furthermore, "scholars" won't go into feelings by any means and discuss the actualities.

Presently when you read this, it may appear as though scholars are the best sort to be in, yet it indeed relies on what kind of circumstance. For instance, a considerable lot of the world's best cooks will, in general, be passionate individuals—and that is no fortuitous event because to be excellent in their profession, they have to feel, sense, and experience things. In any case, a specialist ought not to be an exceptionally enthusiastic individual, but instead a scholar. What's more, with regards to directing occupations or positions where relational aptitudes are required, at that point "choosers" are regularly best, since they can sincerely react to someone else's worry, yet they can likewise observe the reasonable side of it. So when you are in a high-stress circumstance, for instance, you could help a passionate individual by saying: "Would you be able to envision how we'll feel about this circumstance quite a while from now, when we think back on this?" This causes them to disassociate themselves from the circumstance.

Contingent on what sort of individual you are conversing with; various methodologies will generally work viably. Likewise, when you need to persuade enthusiastic individuals, utilize enthusiastic words, that get them energetic. Use words like "amazing," "intense," "unprecedented." For "choosers," you can utilize expressions like: "This isn't simply energizing and fun, it additionally bodes well." And for "masterminds," you present the hard certainties. Notice statistics, talk about "unwavering discernment" and "the cool reality."

As should be obvious, it takes some training to figure out how to peruse individuals like a book - yet once you become acquainted with this, you can without much of a stretch utilize this information to control other individuals.

Personality Psychology

Personality brain science is the investigation of individual contrasts between conduct and thinking. We consider individuals having remarkable characters, and we have words to portray them-your companion is decent, your instructor is mean, your more youthful sibling is timid, etc. When you dive further into personality, it's much more intricate than single word characteristics or even a few attributes set up together. Your companion is decent to you; however, would she say is pleasant to her most noticeably awful foe? Your instructor is mean, yet how can he act with his better half and youngsters? Your more youthful sibling is bashful; however, how can he work inside the home and within sight of just your family? Our characters can change contingent upon the circumstance we're in. However, it appears there must be some temperament, or center, or some essential property that separates individuals from others. So what precisely establishes personality? This is the thing that personality brain research attempts to dissect, find, and clarify. Above all else, personality needs to originate from someplace. Nature is thought as something individuals are brought into the world with, something that is "them" and their identity. Surely, personality is exceedingly hereditary: you may wind up displaying similar personality qualities and quirks as your folks, and indistinguishable twins have been appeared to show fundamentally the same as miens. Science can help clarify how individuals think and act, yet others would differ about this being the entire picture. Natural impacts and the decisions we make can likewise greatly affect our characters. A lively tyke may encounter injury and develop to be shy as a grown-up, or he may defeat struggle and grow up to be versatile. Nature, support, and through and through freedom all connect, and it's this interchange seems to shape personality.

The most present hypothesis in personality brain research is the "if… then" profile. It clarifies personality through this model-if an individual is in this circumstance, it enacts specific musings and sentiments, making the individual demonstration in that manner. Everyone has an inside model that comprises what is designated "psychological full of feeling units." They are organized with the goal that an outside occasion initiates individual units, which actuate others, etc. in a chain until it prompts an activity. The intellectual, emotional unit structures we have created rely upon our natural temperament, culture, and circumstance.

The "if… then" profile is an inventive and pervasive model of personality. However, science is an endless procedure, and this model will undoubtedly be adjusted later on. Imagine a scenario in which "if… then" profiles themselves change. This will be tended to with a more up-to-date model, and more up-to-date models will pursue.

Conclusion

In order to analyze people with dark psychology, you have to be able to understand how they think and why they do what they do. But of course, this is not always easy. They operate from a different perspective than the average person, and their originality can be intimidating. But just because it's difficult doesn't mean it can't be done. It can be done, and it is done every day by people just like yourself.

Every individual is analyzed and categorized according to their attitude. Some examples of this are the attitude of a psychopath, sociopath, or narcissist. There are many explanations as to why these people act in such ways, but it all boils down to how they were raised and what they learned in life. Understanding the psychology behind people with dark mentalities will help you understand them better and also teach you about yourself because any effort put into understanding dark individuals will reflect on how you behave too.

If you want to be able to analyze people with dark psychology it is recommended that you start by looking into the darker side of yourself. It is not necessary, but it will help you understand why people can end up being like this in the first place. If you are always judging others for their actions, then maybe it is because deep down inside there are some things in your own life that you do not wish to admit. The dark side of myself is a part of me and I am always learning to accept it and embrace it.

Learning about dark psychology will help you understand that everyone has a dark side. Every person has something in their past that they wish they could take back and change, but it's something they have to learn to live with.

The different ways that a person handles their dark side is what makes them unique and different from the next person. Nothing is perfect; even if you deny your dark side, you will still have it. There are many ways to cope with dark psychology, such as writing your thoughts and feelings down in a journal or simply talking about it. It's important to have someone else to talk to so that you don't keep everything bottled inside yourself.

If you can see the good in everyone and find the positive in every bad situation, then that is a talent that can be used to their advantage. Being able to tap into your own emotions can be a way of helping others express their emotions. It can be intimidating to talk about these things with other people, so maybe you could start by talking out loud to yourself in the bathroom mirror or while driving your car. But the point is, you should talk about it because this is the first step in learning to accept your dark side and also accept others for who they are.

Writing down your thoughts will help you deal with your dark side. Having a dark side isn't a bad thing; it is just different from most people. People can be judgmental to those who do not share the same beliefs as them, but it is important to remember that everyone has their own way of thinking, feeling, and seeing life. We are all different, but different is not a bad thing.

There are many reasons why people turn out to be the way they are, and it has nothing to do with their intelligence. Intelligence does not have anything to do with your personality; it all comes down to how we grow up and how we were taught as children.

Dark people have a different perspective on life than those who are considered mainstream, and this is something I find fascinating, especially when these people relate the way they think to me. It's not that I like being around dark people all the time, but I do like how they think and explain their perspectives. I'm always impressed by individuals who can get inside someone's head and figure out what makes them tick.

It is important to understand people with dark personalities because there will be moments when you have to deal with them as a part of your job or as a part of your everyday life. They will make you question your own beliefs, so you mustn't be judgmental towards them.